8000 METRES

CLIMBING THE WORLD'S
HIGHEST MOUNTAINS

ALAN HINKES

8000 METRES
CLIMBING THE WORLD'S HIGHEST MOUNTAINS

FOREWORD – BRIAN BLESSED

SHOOTING THE SUMMITS – JOE CORNISH

Printed and bound by KHL Printing, Singapore

Thanks to Vertebrate Publishing for permission to reproduce the quotation from *Upon that Mountain* on page 175.

Lose your dreams
and you will lose your mind.

Jagger/Richards

Published by Cicerone Press
Juniper House, Murley Moss
Oxenholme Road, Kendal
Cumbria LA9 7RL
United Kingdom
www.cicerone.co.uk

Front cover

An early-morning view of K2 from Broad Peak. A ribbon of cirrus cloud often forms on K2 around this level, about 7800m. The final 800m pyramid of K2 rises majestically above the cloud layer.

Back cover (main photo)

Final camp at 8350m on the North Ridge of Everest 8848m. Above the Yellow Band on the North East Ridge, the First Step can be made out – looking like a pimple on the skyline, just right of centre. The Second and Third Steps lead to the summit pyramid.

Back cover (inset photo)

Holding a photo of my daughter, Fiona, on the summit of Nanga Parbat 8125m.

Frontispiece

Kangchenjunga: negotiating deep crevasses on the Great Shelf 7000m, during my attempt in 2000. Later I made a solo push but the risk of avalanches eventually forced me to retreat and I fell into a crevasse, breaking my arm.

Opposite title page

Penitentes on the K2 Glacier create an icy wonderland. Trekking towards Base Camp and the 3000m North Face of K2, China.

pages 190–191

Karakoram, Pakistan: Chogolisa and Masherbrum (K1) above Concordia, the confluence of the Baltoro and Godwin Austen Glaciers, seen from high on Broad Peak.

page 192

Himalaya, Nepal: The moon rises over the North Face of Annapurna 8091m as the summit catches the last rays of the sun.

CONTENTS

ACKNOWLEDGEMENTS

It is humbling that so many people have encouraged and helped me with this book. There are far too many to name check individually so let me begin with a big thank you to you unsung heroes.

To the many people with whom I have shared the hills and climbed routes, often experiencing epics along the way, 'Cheers' for the great mountain days. To my many sponsors over the years who made it all possible: your help is greatly appreciated, thank you.

My Grandma deserves a mention – she put up with her grandson risking his life for months on end in the last years of hers – as does Fiona, my daughter, whose Dad disappeared for long periods of time while she was growing up. I kept in touch on early expeditions by hiring mail runners and persuading passing trekkers to deliver letters, progressing to satellite phones and hefty bills on later ones.

Captain Peter Jackson sorted me out when I suffered a prolapsed disc on Nanga Parbat. Keith Wickham got me cycle training after my leg wound on Makalu. David Thomasson made some great documentaries along with Graham Marples, who also nudged me to get writing. Keith and Joan Cook were there to share and enjoy my success along with Pasang Gelu.

Les Simm was a great help in Kathmandu on my final expeditions and Bikrum Pandey has been there for me for most of them. Thanks also to Paul Havery and Dave Picken for IT support and encouragement, Ian Mulingani for letting me wash up and Lloyd Murray for his enthusiasm.

Joe Cornish's superlative landscape photographs are an inspiration to me and Joe and Jenny took an enthusiastic interest in my own mountain images.

A special thanks has to go to Mike and Marian Parsons for their hospitality and genuine enthusiasm for the book; without them I do not know what would have become of this book, or me; my simple thanks are not enough. Thanks also to my publisher, Jonathan Williams at Cicerone, for his patience over the years.

Finally to my grandchildren, Jay and Mia, for spreading sunshine and happiness in the way that only grandchildren can.

ALAN HINKES

Alan Hinkes

Looking back along the ridge from the summit of Shisha Pangma, at 8046m.
My climbing partner Steve Untch is gasping for air in the rarefied atmosphere.
I wait and photograph the Himalayan sunset before catching him up.

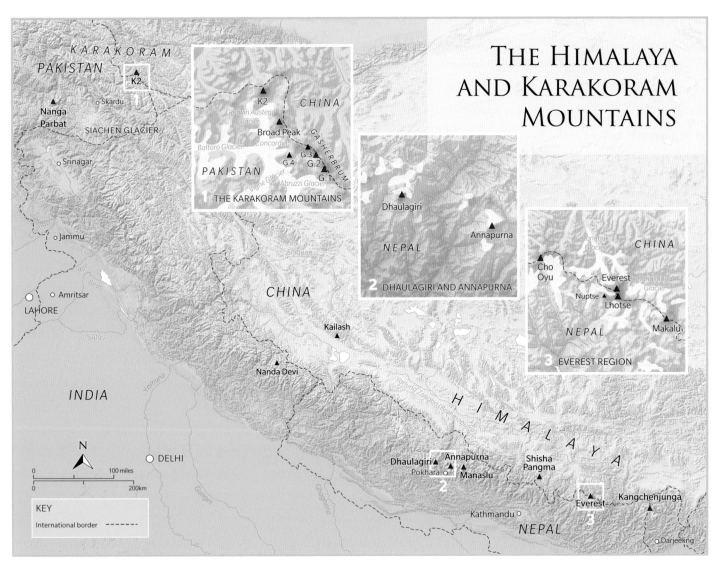

THE HIMALAYA AND KARAKORAM MOUNTAINS

THE KARAKORAM MOUNTAINS

2 DHAULAGIRI AND ANNAPURNA

3 EVEREST REGION

KEY

International border   - - - - -

N

0   100 miles
0   200km

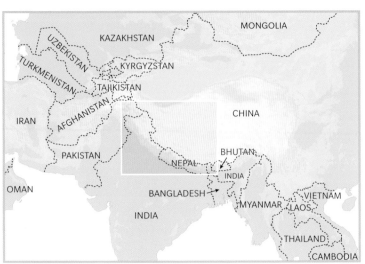

Stripped bare by jet stream winds, the snowless summit ridge of Dhaulagiri was not what I was expecting at over 8000m. Crampons scratch and skitter over the exposed rock as Pasang Gelu sets off down from the summit.

Brian Blessed relaxes
on Everest's North
Col, at 7000m, during
his intrepid bid for
the summit in 1996.

FOREWORD

What a privilege to write the foreword for a book by such a remarkable man as Alan Hinkes. How does one appraise such a character?

This book is a celebration. It is a tale of extraordinary courage and sustained and tenacious endeavour. Books about intrepid adventures and explorers have always fired my imagination and left me begging for more. Such people are our dreams made flesh and blood. Alan fits the bill perfectly; he is the personification of the spirit of adventure.

It is hard to envisage the vast scale of the Himalaya and Karakoram. This is a land of astonishing and gigantic mountains, most of them higher than any other peaks in the rest of the world and Alan Hinkes is the only Briton to summit the 14 highest, all above 8000m.

In 1996 I climbed with him on the north side of Everest and we actually enjoyed suffering together on that cold dangerous mountain where Mallory and Irvine disappeared.

One evening I made my way down the Rongbuk Glacier and became enveloped in darkness on steep hazardous terrain. Fortunately Alan arrived behind me with a torch and painstakingly guided me down to safety and I am deeply grateful to him.

Many factors of awe-inspiring magnitude face those who seek adventure among the highest peaks: climbing difficulties and avalanches; vertical scale; climatic conditions; and frightful altitude problems! The brain has a well-known intolerance for lack of oxygen, mountain sickness with acute pulmonary and cerebral oedema being the major problems. On Everest I witnessed several deaths and permanent damage to body and brain as a result of anoxia. Driven and highly motivated, Alan subjected himself for extended periods to all of these risks. With supreme courage he coped with fatigue, cold, insomnia, diminished appetite and psychogenic stress. He transcended it all to the astonished admiration of both his fellow climbers and the nation.

His amazing photographs tell it all. The great white sweep of the Himalaya! A never-ending ocean of colossal resplendent mountains, blinding in their brilliance as they reach out to a cobalt blue sky. Alan writes as he talks, with passion and simplicity, building on a natural knack for storytelling. He conveys fantastic images of wild landscapes full of vast ridges, an array of colours, deep yawning crevasses and intimidating precipices.

People frequently ask me why climbers keep going from mountain to mountain. I am woefully unable to answer. I cannot fathom the innermost thoughts of the climbing fraternity. But one thing is certain – Alan does not have a death wish. Quite the contrary, he has a life wish. He has determination, an inner strength, a delightful sense of humour and a love of all that is worthwhile. I admire him for it.

The man is truly a legend! His staggering achievement is a clarion call to all who wish to fulfil their dreams. He bellows: 'Nothing is impossible!'

I salute my fellow Yorkshireman.

BRIAN BLESSED

Camels in the Shaksgam River, 1994. This route, explored by Francis Younghusband in 1887, is a long and hazardous approach to the north side of K2 in China. Negotiating the flooded river in summer, when the vast, braided torrent covers most of the valley floor, carries a serious risk of being swept away.

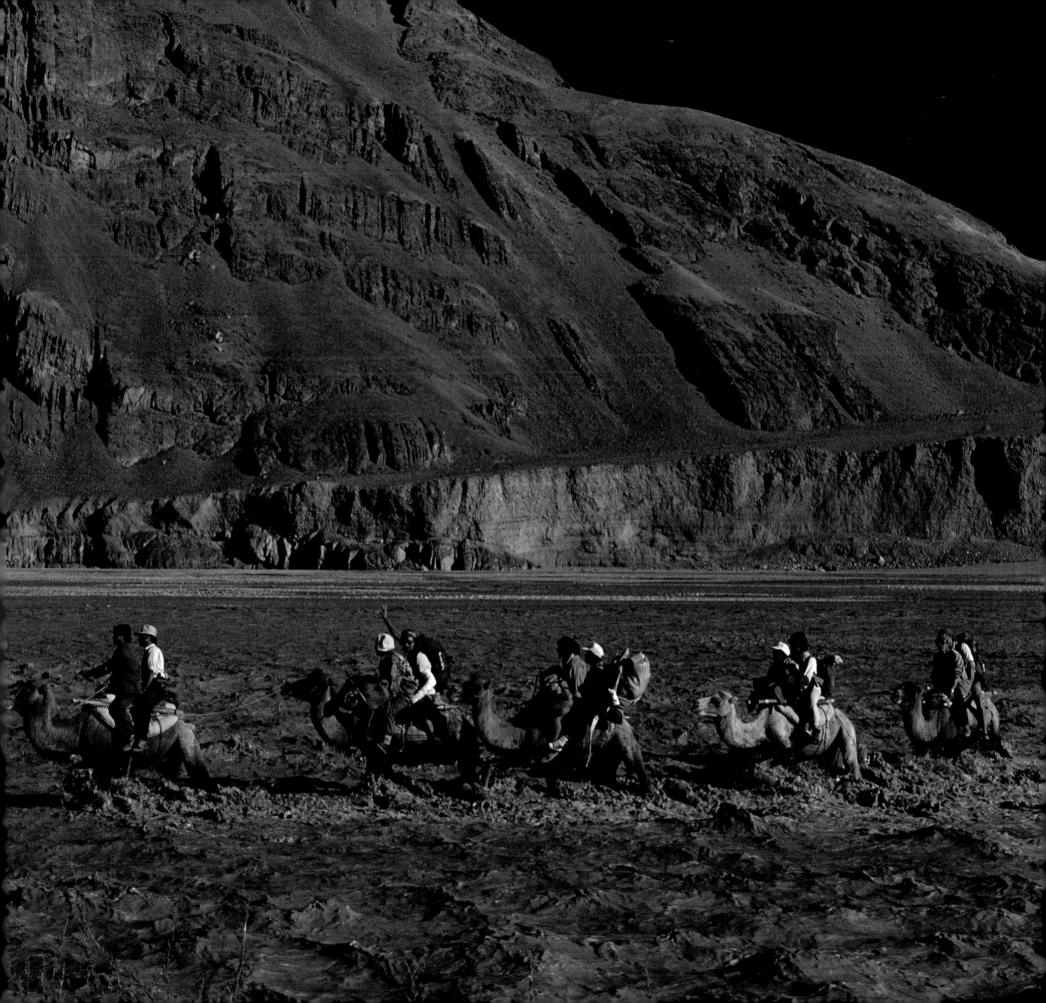

Until one is committed there is hesitancy, the chance to draw back, always ineffectiveness. Concerning all acts of initiative (and creation), there is one elementary truth, the ignorance of which kills countless ideas and splendid plans: that the moment one definitely commits oneself, then Providence moves too. All sorts of things occur to help one that would never otherwise have occurred. A whole stream of events issues from the decision, raising in one's favour all manner of unforeseen incidents and meetings and material assistance, which no man could have dreamt would have come his way. I have learned a deep respect for one of Goethe's couplets:

Whatever you can do, or dream you can, begin it.
Boldness has genius, power, and magic in it.

WH Murray, *The Scottish Himalayan Expedition*

PREFACE

This book is a snapshot of my personal 18-year quest to climb all 14 of the 8000m peaks and tells the story of my ascents of the highest mountains in the world. There were many other expeditions and climbs during that period, but only the Himalayan and Karakoram giants are documented in this book.

Initially I did not plan to tackle them all. I just wanted to climb some of the highest most challenging mountains out there. Over the years it gradually became an odyssey and a test of my resilience, stamina and determination and once I had knocked eight of them off I decided to go for the final six. I made 27 attempts before I succeeded in standing on all 14 summits; some I climbed on my first try, others took three attempts as I often decided to retreat rather than risk everything in a do-or-die assault. Over that 18-year period I would be away every year on at least one and usually two or more expeditions. It was a huge commitment, but it was where I wanted to be.

Many people have pestered me over the years to write a book about climbing the 8000ers, but there was never enough superglue to keep me stuck to a chair in front of a computer to get it done. I was always more interested in going out to play, climbing and being in the hills and I kept putting it off. Sorting out the thousands of photographs and writing the copy was a huge and detailed task, but it was a labour of love, bringing back great memories of friends, climbing mates, epics, gnarly adventures and summits. I took almost every shot myself, often with a self-timer. Sometimes I wonder how I managed to do it in a pre-digital age, carrying many rolls of film and fiddling with manual cameras in bitter cold conditions at extreme altitude.

Now the book is finished, I can go back out to play and enjoy myself in the hills, or perhaps start writing another...

Jay and Mia, my two grandchildren, are the future. I hope they will appreciate the photos and climbing stories in their grandad's book.

Everest (left) and Cho Oyu (right) from the village of Tingri at 4300m on the Tibetan Plateau.

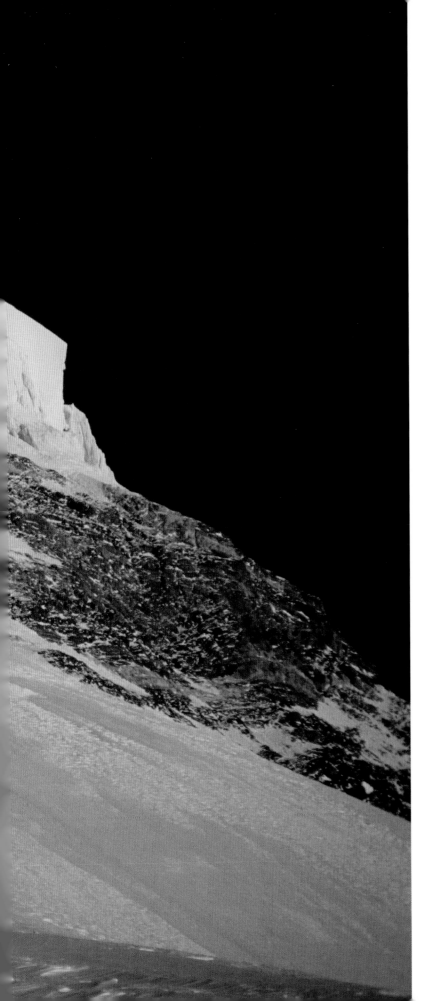

INTRODUCTION

K2: Setting off from the Shoulder at 8000m in the early morning. Looking up towards the Bottleneck – a narrowing couloir topped by a band of huge threatening seracs. These massive ice cliffs look like the White Cliffs of Dover but are rather less friendly. The route, up and left beneath them, is very dangerous as huge sections can – and do – collapse, wiping out anyone below.

I have always been adventurous. As a child I was outside at every opportunity, 'raking about' as they say in Yorkshire, exploring the becks, woods and fields near where I lived in Northallerton. On family drives into the Yorkshire Dales or the North York Moors I felt attracted to the wild, rugged hilly landscape. In my teens, when the chance came to take up climbing on trips with Northallerton Grammar School, the seed was well and truly sown and it very quickly germinated into a passion, eventually becoming a way of life. I knew from the first time that I went out on the moors and fells that it was where I wanted to be. It was a kind of 'calling'.

Going out into the hills of Northern England was an exciting adventure, especially in bad weather. It often seemed to be wet and windy and I quickly learned to cope with and enjoy inclement conditions. In real terms it was more committing than today if only because, in those days before GPS and mobile phones, you had to be more self-reliant. I relished the physical exertion as well as learning the skills of survival and navigation using an Ordnance Survey map and compass. Geography was my favourite subject and to this day I find maps interesting; you could say that I enjoy a good map read. I had a natural talent and quickly became competent at finding my way in the hills, even in poor visibility. I delighted in the challenge of navigating in bad weather and would often go out on the North York Moors in thick hill fog and rain just for fun, to practise map, compass and navigation skills. The vagaries of dense cloud, rain and wind out on the hills and fells did not put me off. I enjoyed the battle against the elements.

Sometimes, just for fun, I would go out onto the moors for a survival experience and spend a night in a 'bivvy bag' – a heavy-duty plastic bag, about the size of a sleeping bag. I learned about exhaustion, exposure and hypothermia, and developed an innate resilience that has served me well.

Tents on Everest's North Col
7000m in 1996. To the right
is the slope that drops to the
East Rongbuk Glacier and
Advance Base Camp 6400m.

You might have an uncomfortable night, you might be shivering, but as long as you can protect yourself from the wind you will at least survive. Later, I practised bivouacking on small ledges, 25 metres up cliff faces. Cramped on such rocky eyries, I had to be tied on all night. Although I was then still at school, I knew that this would be good practice for the bigger mountain faces I would one day climb. Even then, I saw myself ascending Alpine peaks and difficult big walls, such as the North Face of the Eiger, although the Himalaya seemed an unattainable dream.

Progressing from hill walking on the North York Moors, my first mountain was Helvellyn in the Lake District, which I ascended along the rocky knife-edged ridge known as Striding Edge. The topography was a revelation. The peak was like a giant page out of my Physical Geography textbook. In a corrie below the steep summit slopes of Helvellyn there is a small lake called Red Tarn, the last remnant of a melted glacier. Rocky arêtes cradle Red Tarn, Striding Edge to the south and Swirral Edge to the north. Helvellyn remains one of my favourite hills and the climb via Striding Edge above Red Tarn and descent by Swirral Edge is a classic mountain scramble.

On this first scramble it was a wet, windy day, the rock was slippery and I was nearly blown off the ridge by crosswinds. I did not have a waterproof mountain jacket and instead wore a voluminous plastic cycle cape that acted like a parachute, catching the wind and trying to drag me off the mountainside. The experience did not put me off.

Spindrift spills from above as
we climb the 600m big wall on
the South Face of Manaslu.

My passion for the hills and mountains only grew stronger and I wanted more. I yearned for bigger, more testing challenges.

My first rock climbing forays were on sandstone outcrops such as Scugdale and the Wainstones on the North York Moors. I joined the local Cleveland Mountaineering Club, which gave me access to the wisdom of older more experienced climbers as well as lifts to the crags and weekends away. I was fortunate to live close enough to these outcrops to start my climbing outdoors, on real rock. Nowadays many climbers get their first taste of the sport on indoor walls. After learning in relative safety, climbing outside can come as a shock, especially on a cold or wet day.

My first climbs on those 10m faces in North Yorkshire were memorable. It was school winter term and the rock was bitterly cold, with snow lying. My fingers grew numb from touching and gripping holds, causing excruciating pain as they warmed and the blood began to flow through them again. Climbers refer to such re-warming pain as 'heat aches' or 'hot aches'. I have now experienced it a lot more and sometimes the pain has been so intense that I have nearly vomited, but at least I know that I have prevented frostbite by keeping my digits warm.

Longer, more serious routes on the 35m limestone crags of Peak Scar and Whitestone Cliff caught my eye next. Here, I could stretch the rope out and experience more 'exposure' – the term climbers use for the drop below you as you climb. Controlling anxiety and fear when in such exposed positions, high above the ground, is an essential element of rock climbing. I extended my climbing into the Pennines and Yorkshire Dales, on gritstone crags such as Brimham Rocks and Almscliff Crag, as well as limestone faces including Malham Cove and Goredale Scar. In the Lake District I climbed on the big multi-pitch mountain crags, mostly composed of rough, volcanic rocks. As I progressed from hill walking to the steeper terrain of vertical and overhanging rock routes, I felt a frisson at the greater risk and danger. I wanted to experience more serious climbs, push my limits, flirt with that frisson.

The Scottish Highlands in winter was the next step. There I learned the techniques of snow and ice climbing, using crampons and ice axes, as well as survival skills such as snow holing, coping with bad weather and avalanche awareness. In winter the daylight hours are short in Scotland, which focuses the mind on early starts, on speed and efficiency in the hills and on being prepared for 'benightment' – getting caught out after dark. Often the weather can be grim, with gale-force wind, snow and thick cloud reducing visibility and increasing the risk of cold. Avalanches are a real threat in the Scottish Highlands and being able to navigate and survive in such severe conditions is an excellent apprenticeship for the Greater Ranges. Serious and committing mountaineering adventures can be experienced even on the relatively low Scottish mountains in winter. Conditions can be arctic and the hills should not be underestimated. Learning to cope with poor visibility, gale-force winds, blizzards and darkness on a 900–1000m Scottish mountain is excellent practice. Such early testing experiences – minor 'epics', as climbers call them – certainly stood me in good stead for what was to come. If the hill fog socked in on a Himalayan summit, as happened on Cho Oyo and Annapurna, or I ended up descending an 8000er after sunset, as on K2, Nanga Parbat and Kangchenjunga, I was not as anxious as I might have been; my mind had been conditioned, my resilience honed by such earlier mountain experiences in Britain. I still head out to battle blizzards on British hills; there is something satisfying and refreshing about tackling desperate winter weather, when hills that are easy under summer conditions become serious mountains.

To satisfy my desire for bigger hills, I progressed to the Alps, where I climbed classic big routes such as the Matterhorn, Mont Blanc and the North Face of the Eiger. In the Alps I first experienced the unpleasant effects of altitude and it slowed me down, but after a couple of weeks I found that my body acclimatised well and I could soon climb high Alpine routes at virtually full power.

Although I had climbed technically more difficult Alpine routes, the North Face of the Eiger – the Eigerwand – was

Climbing fixed ropes in spindrift conditions
on Broad Peak's steep snow slopes.

Climbing with Doug Scott on a 5000m peak in 1988. This is an acclimatisation climb above Advance Base Camp with Makalu West Face behind.

the big prize for me. I had read so much about that famous, dangerous climb that I felt I was climbing a vertical mountain history book. It was like being on a giant tombstone, passing places where so many climbers had died. The whole experience on that historic north wall was exciting and pleasurable. I seemed able to keep my fear at bay and relish simply being there. I enjoyed the sustained technical mixed snow, ice and rock climbing and was neither particularly fazed nor scared by the fusillade of rocks and stones that whizzed and screeched down the face. These stones are melted out of the summit ice field when the sun reaches it in the late afternoon. Any one of them could have been as lethal as a bullet but it all just seemed part of the experience. Today I would flinch at the sound of each whining, falling rock. Satiating my desire to climb the Eigerwand was a release and the ascent was a rite of passage.

At the time I was working as a teacher and the long summer holiday allowed plenty of time for the ascent. Returning to school that autumn, I remember feeling very satisfied and somehow different from the other teachers who had probably been to the seaside. It was not a feeling of superiority, rather a growing understanding of what

Jerzy Kukuczka, the great Polish mountaineer, in Kathmandu, 1987. Climbing Shisha Pangma, his final 8000m peak, made him the second person to complete all 14 after Reinhold Messner.

I wanted to do in life, a dawning realisation that my approach to life was different. My real ambition was to climb more mountains and not to be stuck in a classroom with only weekends and limited holidays in which to fulfil my passion.

In the mid-1980s I resigned from teaching, took up Himalayan climbing and qualified as a British Mountain Guide, an international accreditation coordinated by the

Camping at 8000m on the north side of K2, the exposed 'Eagle's Nest' bivouac on a tiny rocky ledge below the final hanging glacier which leads to the summit. There is a 2500m drop to Base Camp.

International Federation of Mountain Guide Associations. I could now make my living in the mountains, especially the Alps. While Alpine mountaineering is more dangerous than British climbing – there are rock falls, avalanches, crevasses and dramatic electrical storms – I was not deterred; in fact, I wanted more.

By now, I felt that I had served my apprenticeship in the mountains. I was ready for the Greater Ranges. My first forays were to 5000m and 6000m mountains such as Mount Kenya by the Diamond Couloir, Kilimanjaro by the Heim Glacier, Denali (Mount McKinley), the Andes and many 6000m Himalayan peaks. Here I made several first ascents; I also had a few epics and experienced the effects of increasingly high altitudes on my body.

Climbing on the 8000m peaks felt like a natural progression. It just felt right. My initial attempts were on expeditions I had been invited to join – the first two were on Polish expeditions with the legendary 8000m climber Jerzy Kukuczka, Wanda Rutkiewicz and Krzysztof Wielicki, followed by expeditions with Doug Scott, Benoit Chamoux and other well-known Himalayan climbers – although I later organised my own expeditions.

How did I end up climbing 8000m peaks, on which death can come so easily? I had no plan or desire to climb all 14. It hardly seemed a realistic goal when only two people, Kukuczka and Reinhold Messner, had achieved it. I was simply interested in climbing 8000m mountains because I felt they were the ultimate test of resilience, stamina, skill and endurance.

Climbing 'Alpine-style' on Makalu at 7500m in a one-piece down suit and duvet jacket, in 1988. Lhotse 8516m, the South Col 7920m and Everest 8848m behind. Strapped to my rucksack is a yellow foam Karrimat to insulate me from the snow when bivvying. The ski poles are to help on easier-angled slopes, and to use as probes to check for hidden crevasses. Trekking poles were not common in 1988 and I set a precedent when I used old ski poles. Most people use purpose-made trekking poles now.

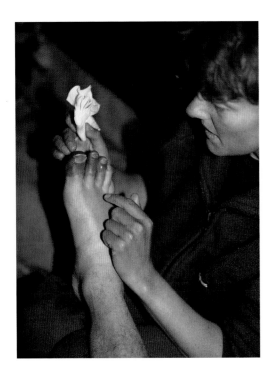

The black frostbitten toes of a climber I rescued from K2. Subsequently these three toes were amputated.

All of the 8000ers are in what is dubbed 'the death zone', an unforgiving environment in which your body starts to deteriorate to the point at which you actually start to die. It is not possible for a human being to survive for long beyond a couple of days above 8000m and there are no rescue teams or helicopters to rely on. A helicopter has an operational ceiling of 6500m. Simply surviving takes tremendous effort, both physically and mentally. All water, which you must drink to prevent dehydration and stay alive, is frozen as snow and ice and requires laborious effort melting it on a small stove. Breathing and movement are difficult and slow, sleep is virtually impossible and the cold, often 40 below, will freeze exposed flesh. Frostbite is a real possibility, often leading to the loss of frozen fingers, toes or even limbs.

Between 8000m peak expeditions I was usually in Britain, the Alps or climbing other 6000m and 7000m Himalayan peaks. Working as an International Mountain Guide meant that my world revolved around mountains. Climbing one 8000er, I realised, had been a privilege but I developed an urge to test myself on a few more.

My first sighting of K2 from Concordia in the Karakoram made a great impression on me. I knew that I had to climb that stark, dramatic steep-sided peak, known as the Savage Mountain. My quest for its summit extended over three expeditions; I dedicated, or possibly donated, three years of my life to that mountain. And after filming on the summit of K2, proving I could handle a camera at 8000m, I was then invited on Everest as a cameraman.

Eventually, in 1996, I realised that I had climbed eight 8000ers including the hardest, K2, and the highest, Everest. The following year I decided that, as I was more than half way, I might as well attempt the remaining six. The decision was not as casual as that makes it sound; it was more a gradual dawning that, with tremendous effort and determination, ascending them all would be a worthy and achievable goal.

It is a quantifiable challenge in mountaineering, just as the four-minute mile is a quantifiable challenge in athletics.

From then on I generally organised my own lightweight, Alpine-style expeditions, including several solo climbs. It took me another eight years to summit all 14 of the 8000m peaks. Some I climbed on my first attempt; on others I backed off and tried another year. Just surviving an attempt on an 8000m peak is a success and my view has always been that there is no failure in retreat as the mountain will always be there. I can always return. Geoffrey Winthrop Young wrote in his classic 1920s book *Mountain Craft*: 'In climbing mountains, danger is a constant element, not remote as in other sports: it is always with us behind the veil of pleasant circumstances, and it can be upon us before we are aware.'

In the end it took 27 expeditions before I had climbed all 14 and I class them all as successes. Pushing on regardless and getting killed, or suffering severe frostbite that results in amputation, is failure. No mountain is worth a digit and I have so far kept all mine. Many high-altitude mountaineers and 8000m summiteers have had toes or fingers amputated after frostbite. I learnt a lot from Polish climbing friends on some of my early expeditions. Quite a few had toes missing and they encouraged me to look after mine as they wished they had done theirs. It was poignant and salutary advice. Attention to detail is very important when climbing any mountain, rock or ice face, especially if you are to stay alive and avoid frostbite.

At that time, much of my life was spent away on expeditions. An 8000m peak attempt can last three months UK-to-UK; one trip to the remote north side of K2 took five months. Usually I would spend a week in Kathmandu or Islamabad obtaining a permit from the Ministry of Tourism, clearing the expedition cargo through customs, organising equipment, food, porters and generally planning the next several weeks. The trek in to Base Camp often lasts between 10 and 12 days, after which it's best to spend three weeks acclimatising by climbing higher on the mountain and returning to Base Camp to recover. Once you have acclimatised it may still be two or more weeks' wait for a clear weather window in which to climb safely. The summit climb itself might only take between one

and four days, depending on difficulty, with another day or two to descend. Then, when you leave Base Camp, the trek out could take five days, unless you can afford a helicopter.

Finding British mountaineers willing to commit the time necessary for an 8000m expedition became difficult. On my final 8000m climbs I was joined by one of my Nepalese friends, Pasang Gelu, a great character with the kind of relaxed personality that is essential for coping with the strains of extreme altitude. Pasang had a genuine desire to climb big Himalayan peaks, was easy to get along with and we made a good team.

Climbing is a way of life for me; I am addicted. If you were to cut me in half, you would find 'mountain climber' written all the way through. I love being in the hills and the biggest hills of the Himalaya and Karakoram, being the most dangerous, offer the greatest challenge. But I do not climb to die. I climb to live – and climbing enhances my life.

Over my 18-year quest to climb the 8000m peaks, I have always stuck to my motto: 'No mountain is worth a life, coming back is a success and the summit is only a bonus.'

Main photo

Early morning, setting off from the Shoulder at over 8000m on K2. A Dutch climber follows me up towards the Bottleneck.

Inset photo

A Twin Otter and a Russian Mi-17 heli at Lukla airstrip, the start of the Everest and Lhotse Base Camp treks through Nepal's Khumbu region. It is an exciting landing and take-off; the airstrip is not much bigger than an aircraft carrier, perched on the mountainside.

The North Face of Shisha Pangma, from the Tibetan Plateau at 4500m. My new route in 1987 took the central gully line, slanting right-to-left up the face, to the notch in the ridge before the prominent central summit.

1 SHISHA PANGMA

8046M, 1987

Snow was melting in a small pan over a mini gas burner. Steve Untch, my 6'5" American climbing mate, was doing his best to relax, despite being crammed into the little space remaining in our tiny bivvy tent. Close by in another tent, Jerzy 'Jurek' Kukuczka and Artur 'Słoń' Hajzer were also brewing up. We were at around 6500m on Shisha Pangma and the purring stoves and steaming water heralded refreshment. I was in my element and where I wanted to be, in the Himalaya on an 8000m peak. As I contemplated the warm mug of tea, all thought of danger was washed to the back of my mind.

Abruptly, I was snapped out of this blissful reverie by an ominous, alarmingly loud thud and portentous rumble. Suddenly it was 'action stations'. There was a great cacophony of yelling in both English and Polish, and I heard Artur and Jurek screaming, 'Avalanche! Run! Get Out! Avalanche! Come On! Avalanche!'

I pushed the stove out of the door and the precious water spilled over the snowy ground as I frantically yanked my boots on.

In the ensuing chaotic melée I felt Steve clambering over me as he desperately tried to squeeze his huge body out of the constriction of the tent door at the same time as Jurek was gallantly trying to drag me out. It would have been comical if it had not been so terrifyingly serious. It felt like being ambushed and having to scramble and dive for cover, yet in a jubilant, mock-heroic way I was enjoying the drama. Gasping in the icy cold thin air, we tumbled down the easy-angled snow slope below the tent as the soft slab avalanche slithered down towards us.

Fortunately the avalanche ground to a halt before reaching our tents and we literally gulped sighs of relief in the rarefied air; it had been a near miss. When we had all recovered enough to stop blaspheming, I thanked Jurek for his selfless bravery in helping me out of my tent when he could have scurried away. It was a brutal baptism and a great revelation. I now clearly understood that I was not just out for a jolly jaunt with the mountaineering legend Jerzy Kukuczka. Escaping the avalanche heightened my senses and reminded me that I was in a highly hazardous, unforgiving environment. I learned a lot about how to stay alive in the Himalaya on this expedition, especially from Jurek and Artur, and it was to stand me in good stead on many future trips. Ironically, and to my great sadness, Jurek was killed only two years later on the South Face of Lhotse.

We had travelled out to Tibet – a mystical, elusive country – and Shisha Pangma seemed an obscure and enigmatic mountain. I was part of a post-monsoon Polish international expedition, organised by the Katowice Mountain Club. I had effectively served an 'apprenticeship' climbing and learning how to survive on 5000m and 6000m peaks in both the Andes and the Himalaya and was now embarking on an adventure to tackle this giant peak with some of the best high-altitude mountaineers in the world. The audacious plan was to attempt two 8000m peaks in succession – first a new route on Shisha Pangma and then the unclimbed South Face of Lhotse, a technical, steep Himalayan 'big wall'.

We left Kathmandu in late August and headed up the Friendship Highway to Tibet, in the People's Republic of China. As well as Jurek and Artur, other team members included Wanda Rutkiewicz (Poland), Christine de Colombel (France), Ramiro Navarette (Ecuador), Carlos Carsolio (Mexico) and my climbing partner Steve Untch.

Mud and rockslides caused by monsoon rains blocked the road in many places, and we had to walk most of the way to the Nepal–Tibet border. It was very hot and humid so we often stopped to cool off in the many waterfalls and plunge pools along the way. We soon lost our inhibitions and got to know each other fairly well. The French female contingent fearlessly led the skinny-dipping, rapidly followed by the British and US contingent (Steve and myself). As you would.

Crossing the border from Kodari in Nepal to Zhangmu in Tibet was a curious experience but uneventful. We lodged in the so-called best hotel in town, a scruffy concrete multi-storey building. The TVs did not work and the en suite bathrooms in each bedroom were not plumbed in. Instead there was a squalid porcelain-tiled communal toilet room with a slit in the floor and a big stick to poke the solids down. There was no dining room in the hotel but further up the street a 'restaurant' perched on the edge of the Bhote Khosi gorge served palatable food and excellent bottled Chinese beer. To our amazement, after each course most of the plates, the left-over food and all the empty bottles were thrown out of the window into the gorge. Looking down we could see a huge pile of broken bottles and rubbish.

We travelled by Land Cruiser to a roadhead base camp at 5000m, stopping at villages such as Nyalam for a few days' acclimatisation en route. The Tibetan Plateau was a complete contrast to the hot, humid Nepalese lowlands. Here it was clear, bright, sunny weather and sunburn was a problem, although the nights were icy cold. We hired yaks to take us up to 5900m and the nomadic yak herders arrived to meet us as if by magic, emerging from the barren Tibetan wilderness. Exuding an aroma of smoky yak excrement tinged with rancid yak butter, they certainly looked like proper Tibetans, with jet-black, shiny, plaited hair; most of them were dressed in woollen felt and animal-skin clothes and bootees. To us they were wild-looking characters, but to them we climbers in our modern

avalanche. But 8000m was a new concept. We could hardly have started our summit attempt in a more naïve fashion, planning our Alpine-style ascent without fixed ropes or a tent. I can barely believe we got away with only taking Gore-Tex bivi bags for the final push. We were incredibly lucky and this was the last time I went so high without taking some kind of bivouac shelter.

As so often happens in the Himalaya, the weather broke and we were holed up at Base Camp for over a week in cold, murky conditions with fresh snowfall most days. I didn't get bored or even frustrated, as there was plenty of vodka and general craic to be had with the expedition team. By mid-September the weather started to clear and, seizing the opportunity, we left Base Camp. Our overloaded, heavy rucksacks, with equipment strapped to the sides, weighed more than 20kg making it an arduous slog up to the bottom of our chosen line, the unclimbed couloir cutting right to left up the north face. Eventually we pitched a tiny bivouac tent in the flattish glacier valley at around 6900m below the north face.

The next day we left the tent behind, intending to collect it on our descent, and started climbing the steepening snow and ice slope in the couloir.

At first, on the easier-angled lower section of the gully, we took turns to break trail. Sometimes the thin frozen crust would collapse and we would sink knee deep into the snow, which was very debilitating.

Upward progress was slow with our heavy rucksacks and as the angle of the slope got steeper, we roped up. The couloir, or gully as it would be called in Scotland, was about grade 3 with steeper sections of hard ice. Technically we were in our comfort zone, but approaching 8000m with our hefty rucksacks we had to dig deep into our reserves of stamina.

The weather remained clear and settled and we climbed until late afternoon before stopping at 7850m to hack out two eyric-like narrow ledges in the 50° snow and ice slope. These uncomfortable perches were all we had to lie on for the night. We had sleeping bags to snuggle into, but covered only by a thin bivi-bag we were still cold when the temperature dropped to -25°C overnight. I was in charge of

fleece and Gore-Tex kit must have seemed like peculiar aliens. Unfortunately they also took a fancy to some of our stuff and we had to guard all our kit and supplies carefully.

Jurek and Artur planned to climb together, attempting a new route, the traverse of the skyline ridge of Shisha Pangma. Steve and I also had our sights on a new route, lightweight and Alpine-style, just the two of us. We had noticed the obvious diagonal ramp line and couloir running right to left up the North Face, starting from a high altitude basin-like glacial valley at 6900m. Wanda later told me that Reinhold Messner had wanted to climb this line in May 1981 but backed off because of deep monsoon snow. It looked like a steep snow climb at first, reminiscent of a giant steep but easy Scottish gully, such as Number 2 Gully on Ben Nevis. However, higher up it became a lot steeper, icier and rockier before it joined the summit ridge that Jurek and Artur would be climbing. The rest of the team were climbing together up the original route first climbed in 1964. Shisha Pangma was the last 8000er to be climbed, mainly because it was in Tibet and until the 1980s western climbers had been refused access.

By the end of August, using our experience of many other climbs up to 6500m, Steve and I had acclimatised to nearly 6800m when we narrowly missed being engulfed in the

trying to melt snow for water, balancing the gas burner and half litre pan on the snow slope. This essential but laborious task was made more difficult by copious waves of spindrift, which would periodically roar down from the summit ridge and engulf us. Spindrift is very fine-grained snow like freezing sand, which penetrates every conceivable orifice. I could not keep the stove going in the cascading spindrift and we had to survive the night on minimal fluids. Several times during the night Steve mentioned that his feet were cold. I massaged and wriggled my toes most of the night. It was more a torture session than rest and recuperation as we suffered and shivered through the freezing bleak night.

As soon as it was light we packed our rucksacks, anxious to leave our tiny, joyless ledges, but we were determined to summit. The final section of the couloir was steep and rocky in places before we broke out onto the ridge at about 8000m. There we found tracks in the snow left by Jurek and Artur who had climbed their new route to the top the previous day. Seeing the footprints in the snow allowed us to be less anxious, as we now had a trail to follow, however the climbing still needed concentration and we could not relax. It was no bimble. We were on a narrow, airy ridge and on both sides there was a thousand metre drop – no place to become complacent.

Steve mentioned his cold feet again, but wanted to push on. I continued scrunching and wriggling my toes at every gruelling step. We toiled up a steep knife-edged snow arête to the Central summit, from where a long and beautiful snow ridge stretched for over a kilometre to the main summit. It was getting late in the day. We were tired, bordering on exhaustion after climbing difficult technical terrain since dawn, but somehow we knew that we had enough in reserve to reach the summit. We pushed on, following Jurek and Artur's tracks in the snow. It was nice to think that Jurek had climbed his final 8000m peak.

Working our way along this ridge, all above 8000m, we knew that we would have to retrace our steps in order to descend; yet it never crossed our minds to cut down early and forgo the summit. We had to reach the highest point of Shisha Pangma. It is what mountaineers do.

When I reached the top I remember sitting down in the soft snow as Steve came up. The evening light was turning the snow a shade of orange, and one side of the ridge was already in shade. After a few photos Steve set off down and I soon caught him up. As we dropped down off the ridge, descending onto the open face of the original 1964 route, the light was fading and we had to struggle down in the dark with dim head torches whose batteries were fading fast. This was in the days before modern lithium batteries and LED head torches. Later that night we found our bivi-tent and I managed to melt some snow for water. It had been a debilitating 48-hour push. Steve removed his boots to find that his feet were swollen and dark purple. I recognised it as deep frostbite, but tried not to alarm him. There was no point in warming his feet at this altitude, which would cause extreme pain and make it even more difficult for him to climb down. Nevertheless, I knew that he had to get down quickly, as this was serious frostbite, needing intensive medical attention.

With some effort we made it to Base Camp 20 hours later, where the experienced Polish doctor Lech Korniszewski expertly tended to Steve's now blackened toes and purple feet. Steve was a big strong 6'5" ex-US Army Master Sergeant but he cried in pain unashamedly as his feet were re-warmed. There was no helicopter to get Steve back to Kathmandu, he had to suffer the ordeal of being carried part of the way, and at times hobble agonisingly on his heels. Once back in the US he had several toes amputated from each foot.

My feet and toes were unscathed. Perhaps I had put more effort into rubbing my feet on the comfortless bivouac ledge, when we had slept out in the open at nearly 8000m. My motto is that no mountain is worth a life, coming back is a success, and the summit is only a bonus. Neither is any mountain worth a digit and I still have all my fingers and toes. Maybe Steve was just unlucky; he did have size 14 feet.

Steve was one of the finest people I have been on a mountain with. He was gallant, selfless and good humoured, all qualities that are essential when you feel exhausted and need to find the inner strength to carry on. Seven years later Steve was courageously helping an injured climber down

K2 when a rope snapped and he fell to his death. He was an unsung hero and always ready to help others. Tragically it cost him his life.

The expedition to Shisha Pangma was a great success. Most of the team climbed the original 1964 route to the top, including Wanda Rutkiewicz, Ramiro Navarette, the first Ecuadorian to climb an 8000er, and Carlos Carsolio, who went on to climb all 14. Steve and I had climbed a new route, perhaps innocently using 6000m peak tactics, but we had got away with it, albeit with Steve's frostbite. But more importantly, 'Jurek' Jerzy Kukuczka climbed his last 8000m peak in fine style, by a new route, with Artur Hajzer. We had a celebration in Base Camp, fuelled by Polish vodka, and then celebrated again back in Kathmandu. Jurek went back to Poland as a national hero, the second person after Reinhold Messner to climb all 14 8000m peaks.

It never entered my head that one day I too might climb them all. At that time only two mountaineers had ever achieved this 'grand slam'. More people had walked on the moon, so it seemed almost unattainable. I just wanted to continue climbing and experience the challenge of giant Himalayan peaks.

After a few days in Kathmandu most of the Shisha Pangma team went home, and I set off with Artur Hajzer and Carlos Carsolio to attempt the huge unclimbed 3000m Big Wall of Lhotse South Face.

JERZY KUKUCZKA &
THE POLISH CLIMBERS

Above

Artur Hajzer, Wanda Rutkiewicz and Jerzy Kukuczka at Shisha Pangma Base Camp, sorting loads for higher up the mountain. The T-shirt slogan has a misprint: it should read 8046m.

Left

The breathtaking summit ridge of Shisha Pangma, looking to the main summit at 8046m. The tracks made by Jerzy Kukuczka and Artur Hajzer the day before are still in the snow for Steve and me to follow to the summit.

Right

Janusz Majer, Carlos Carsolio, Krzysztof Wielicki and Jerzy Kukuczka prepare loads in a Kathmandu hotel room in August 1987. I planned to go directly from the Shisha Pangma expedition to join Wielicki on Lhotse South Face.

We had run out of vodka. Unfazed, the Polish expedition doctor made cocktails with medicinal alcohol and orange juice powder.

Jerzy Kukuczka had just climbed his 14th 8000m peak and we were celebrating in Shisha Pangma Base Camp, Tibet. Having climbed only one 8000er at that time, I was in awe of his achievement. To climb all 14 seemed like going to the Moon.

Kukuczka was unassuming and quietly spoken. In Kathmandu he would smoke and drink whisky every night but stopped smoking on the walk-in to Base Camp. He ate speck (pork) every day and paced himself carefully, acclimatising slowly but surely. He did not rush around or try to make a summit bid before he felt properly acclimatised. I learned a lot from him.

Over the course of the expedition I had got to know and tune in to the Polish attitude. Kukuczka's wicked sense of humour was similar to mine so I could not resist asking him whether he had been to the top of Kangchenjunga. Many climbers stop short of the summit out of respect for the people of Sikkim, who regard the mountain as sacred. His answer in broken, Polish-accented English was emphatic: 'Oh yes! I stomped all over f***ing summit!' I remember wondering what I would do if I ever climbed Kangchenjunga.

My first meeting with Jurek, as his friends called him, was in his Polish hometown of Katowice, in 1987, when Poland was still in the Soviet Bloc. I was visiting as a guest of the High Mountain Club of Katowice and we were heading off to the Tatra Mountains for some winter climbing. Jurek, already a legend, had just returned from the winter ascent of Annapurna, his 13th 8000m peak. Other well-known Polish climbers joined the Anglo-Polish Tatra climbing meet, including Voytek Kurtyka, Wanda Rutkiewicz, Artur Hajzer, Janusz Majer and Krzysztof Wielicki. It was -15°C and the snow was black with Katowice's coal dust and pollution. I could see how the bleak harsh landscape and lifestyle had toughened up these gnarly mountaineers. I enjoyed a couple of winter trips to the Tatra and two Himalayan expeditions with the Poles. I always felt we were on the same wavelength. It seemed as if the British and Polish understood each other. Sadly, Jurek died while attempting a new route on Lhotse in 1989, and Artur died on Gasherbrum I in 2013.

High on the summit slopes of Manaslu, heading for the top.

2 MANASLU

8163M, 1989

In December 1988 my telephone rang. I lifted the handset and a man speaking with a Gallic accent introduced himself as Benoit Chamoux. I was aware of this well-known French mountaineer; he had made his name with a very fast ascent of K2 and had summited several other 8000ers, openly declaring his intention to be the first Frenchman to climb all 14. He was developing quite a reputation among the international mountaineering community and was fast becoming a household name in France. My first reaction to his French-accented voice inviting me to the Himalaya was that it was a hoax call, so I told him where to go and put the phone down. It sounded too good to be true.

Luckily Benoit rang back and persuaded me it really was him. He wanted me to join his L'Esprit d'Equipe team of European mountaineers sponsored by Bull, a French multi-national computer company. Loosely translated, L'Esprit d'Equipe means 'team spirit'. This was a unique and well-funded Himalayan climbing team, with the main aim of climbing 8000m peaks.

I met Benoit on Christmas Eve 1988 at Bull's Paris headquarters. It was soon clear that Benoit's lucrative sponsorship deal was unlike anything I had come across before. Earlier that year I had been on a Chris Bonington-led expedition in Nepal and Tibet, to 'Search for the Yeti'. That was a well-sponsored trip with backing from The Mail on Sunday, William Hill Bookmakers, and the Safeway supermarket chain (now Morrisons). It also involved a BBC film crew making a documentary and hoping we might find the Yeti. Along with Andy Fanshawe, I made the first ascent of Menlungtse West, a 7000m peak. Even that well-underwritten, relatively well-heeled expedition seemed impecunious compared to Benoit's lavish budget. The L'Esprit d'Equipe team members even got a small fee and summit bonus, in addition to all their expenses and expedition costs. Normally I only managed to get a little subsidy and help towards my overall costs for an expedition, in the form of small grants from the Mount Everest Foundation (MEF) and the British Mountaineering Council (BMC). Just occasionally, I was lucky enough to attract sponsorship from a company hoping for some PR, marketing or advertising return. It is more usual for an expedition to demand that your own money be earned, saved and then spent on the trip.

I liked Benoit. He was a professional mountain guide like me and we seemed to click and got on well together. I sensed that we shared a deep passion for mountains and I happily and eagerly signed up as the token Anglo Saxon, or as the French would have it, 'le rosbif'.

As soon as the Paris meeting ended, I set off to catch the last flight from Paris Charles de Gaulle airport back to Britain. What a great Christmas present, I thought. I could hardly believe it. I now had several fully-funded expeditions to look forward to. And to think I had initially put the phone down on Benoit, thinking it was a mate having a laugh.

I was in a joyful, Happy Christmas frame of mind as I boarded the British Airways aeroplane. The pilot cheered me up even more when he announced his name over the intercom: 'Good evening, everyone. This is Captain Kirk speaking.' Everyone expected him to maintain the Star Trek theme and announce that the First Officer was Mr Spock. The roar of laughter must have reached him on the flight deck as he continued his pre-flight spiel, but I suppose he was used to it – he really was Captain Kirk.

L'Esprit d'Equipe required regular commitment. I would travel to France every month, usually to Paris, Chamonix or the Alps. The idea was to keep the team close-knit, train together and bond as well as setting an example for the Bull company employees. Previously Bull had sponsored an ocean-going yacht in the Round the World Race. Benoit decided that a two-day team-building and bonding trip on a racing yacht into the Atlantic from St Malo was a good idea. This was a new and different experience for me, more used to the mountains and terra firma. I had done several sea

kayak trips off the British coast, but this was much further out on the ocean. It required teamwork and commitment in an unforgiving environment and I quickly realised that if I went overboard I would be as dead as if I had fallen down an 8000m mountain face.

The rest of the climbing team was a great bunch of experienced French, Dutch, Italian and Czech mountaineers. It was good to make new friends and practise European harmony. Contrary to many people's expectations, we all got on very well and enjoyed climbing together as well as our bonding and team-building exercises. English was the common language (or the lowest common denominator?) for everyone. In Nepal, English was spoken rather than French or Italian and, apart from the odd curse, very little Czech was uttered. French was generally spoken in Bull meetings in France and I became reasonably competent at speaking and understanding French, which was a useful bonus.

I felt fortunate to be visiting France nearly every month. I made some great French friends and got to know many delightful, amazing places. France has a wealth of varied climbing areas, and as a team we also canoed, hiked and skied together. I enjoyed the French culture – their food, wine

A huge airborne avalanche roaring off Peak 29 towards Manaslu Base Camp.

The air blast reached us like a severe blizzard, covering the tents in snow.

and the French way of life. In the 1980s I did not need to be as politically correct as now and the rosbif's quips about Agincourt, Trafalgar, Waterloo and Dien Bien Phu were taken in the light-hearted spirit in which they were intended.

Benoit set the agenda for the team, which was all about him becoming the first French climber to bag all 14 of the 8000m mountains (something that would never happen – he disappeared on Kangchenjunga in 1995). At the time, I was just happy to be part of a great team, make new friends and climb some big Himalayan hills. At that point Benoit had eight 8000ers under his belt and had decided that Manaslu would be next, which was lucky for me, as, if we were successful, I would be the first Brit to climb it. However, it was not just a matter of Benoit getting to the top; part of the ethos of L'Esprit d'Equipe was to get everyone in the team up to the summit as a conspicuous display of teamwork.

In March 1989 we set off for the south side of the mountain, which very few people attempt to climb even today, not least because of the difficulties in getting there. Once we had left the last village, we had to hack our way through jungle undergrowth, cutting a trekking path with khukris and machetes. It took several days of hard labour rather than the usual bimble along a well-trodden trekking path before we reached the more open glacial area above the tree line. The arduous journey felt eerie, as we were all alone, well off the beaten track. There were no local villagers, teashops or trekking lodges, no other expeditions and no trekkers. There did not even appear to be any wildlife about – we had probably scared it off as we crashed and chopped our way through the pathless forest. Reinhold Messner had made the first ascent of this route with a Tyrolean expedition in 1972. Since then very few people had passed this way. It was almost virgin territory.

Base Camp was a barren spot on the moraine-covered Thulagi Glacier. We cleared and built flat areas like patios for our tents on the rock-strewn ice; some of the platforms had to be quite spacious as we had the latest, luxurious two-metre dome tents to erect. The south face of Manaslu, a massive 600m rock wall, towered above Base Camp and huge

Manaslu Base Camp after heavy snowfall
had damaged some of the tents.

Big wall climbing – 600m of serious technical rock climbing on the South Face of Manaslu.

avalanches poured off the mountain and its neighbour P29 virtually every day. They would often reach Base Camp as blizzards, dusting the area with a layer of fine snow. It was impressive but also somewhat unnerving, as we knew it would only take a slightly bigger avalanche to wipe us all out.

The South Face of Manaslu is a Himalayan 'big wall', involving steep rock climbing at high altitude. Pushing out the route on the huge rock face, I found the lead climbing challenging and satisfying. It was certainly no snow plod. We had to fix ropes and, at one point, we rigged up a cableway, like a mini téléphérique, to transport the team's equipment up the steep rock barrier to the Upper Manaslu South Glacier, nicknamed the Butterfly Valley. This 5km-long glacier-filled valley is like the Western Cwm on Everest, it is exposed to avalanches from surrounding peaks on both sides and leads up to the final summit slopes of Manaslu.

Just crossing the glacier to the bottom of the big wall from Base Camp was like a giant game of Russian roulette, with massive avalanches frequently scouring the route. It was a scary two-hour trek to the relative safety of the rock face. We had to gauge the threat and decide when the next avalanche was likely before moving; if we had been caught out in the open we would have been wiped out. Once an avalanche goes airborne, you can be killed by the pressure wave, a huge blast of air that forges ahead of the roaring snow like an explosion; large avalanches can completely wipe out villages and flatten forests.

During that two-hour approach to the shelter of the wall, I often felt as though I was on a military patrol, constantly looking for the nearest cover of a big boulder or crevasse in case we came under 'effective enemy fire'. In that scenario, the enemy was the constant threat of avalanche and rock fall, which was as lethal as any gunfire or mortar attack. It was always a relief to reach the cover and safety of the South Face. Climbing the vertical and overhanging 600m rock face was the key to the ascent, but not easy at this altitude. Overcoming it took nearly three weeks of effort, determined teamwork and technical rock climbing. Higher up in the Butterfly Valley between 5800m and 6000m the steepness eased and the

The Butterfly Valley (Upper Manaslu's South Glacier). The route
went well to the left to the col, avoiding avalanches from the
hanging glaciers and seracs on the peak's summit slopes.

climbing was back on snow and ice, where in addition to the avalanche danger there were hidden crevasses to cope with. As we made our way up the hanging glacier towards the steep snow and ice slope which led to the summit, the atmosphere was excitably amicable. In a curiously masochistic way, we all relished the challenge of ferrying heavy loads higher up the mountain and setting up a camp ready for the summit push. Our training sessions had instilled in us the 'all for one and one for all' ethic and we worked together well. Originally Himalayan expeditions had involved a team of many climbers pushing higher and higher up a mountain, establishing and stocking camps with equipment and food. When all the tents were in place, usually only two climbers from the group would make the final summit push. The ethos of L'Esprit d'Equipe, to which Benoit and all of us were dedicated, was to get every member to the top, not only as an obligation to our sponsors but also as an illustration of teamwork. Eventually an assault camp was established at about 7400m, leaving a 750m final ascent to the top.

Benoit nabbed a good weather window and reached the summit first, bagging another 8000er for his collection. I was acclimatised, fit and ready for a summit bid with one of the Italians, but we had to retreat as his feet were numb with cold and he was concerned that frostbite was setting in – so we climbed down to warm his toes in the tent. We spent the night keeping as warm as possible, melting snow for water and fuelling up with fluid and calories before making another bid for the top.

True rest is difficult to achieve at high altitude, sleep is fitful and fitness deteriorates. We knew that we had to make another summit bid the next day, so prepared and rested as well as we could. Luckily the weather remained clear and settled and we confidently set off for the summit, this time with no cold feet. The final narrow ridge to the summit with a big drop on either side was much steeper than I expected. I could not let my concentration wander, as one trip or slip would send me sliding thousands of feet to my death. I remember the air being crystal clear and very cold, about -20°C. The views were amazing, it was one of those days when it seemed that you could see forever and I felt

Benoit Chamoux and
Pierre Royer in Base Camp,
satisfied but exhausted.

tremendously privileged just to be there. I managed to get a summit photo of me holding a picture of my daughter, Fiona, who was only a toddler at that time.

The expedition was a great success, no one died and all the L'Esprit d'Equipe climbers made it to the top and back without frostbite or other injury. Bull Computers was very pleased with the publicity and decided to continue the funding. The mountain was first climbed in 1956 from the north side by a Japanese expedition. As an added bonus for me, 33 years after that first ascent, I had become the first Brit to reach the summit.

On the summit of Manaslu,
15 May 1989, holding a photo
of my daughter, Fiona. This was
my second 8000m peak. I never
imagined then that I would go on
to climb them all. In this photo
she is only a child; by the time I
had finished all 14 she was grown
up and had her own little boy.

Where's my pint?
With iconic Italian mountaineer Reinhold Messner, the first person to climb all the 8000m peaks.

REINHOLD MESSNER

Italian mountaineer Reinhold Messner is an icon of almost mythical status. His contribution to mountaineering, especially among the Himalayan and Karakoram 8000ers, is unequivocal. His achievements are a benchmark.

In 1986, he became the first person to have climbed all of the 8000m peaks, one year ahead of Polish climber Jerzy Kukuczka.

Climbing all 14 peaks is a quantifiable and inspirational goal in mountaineering, just as the four-minute mile, first run by a Briton, Roger Bannister, paced by Chris Brasher and Chris Chataway, is in athletics. More than a thousand people have run a four-minute mile since 6 May 1954. So far fewer than 30 have climbed all 14 8000m peaks and it will be a long time before a thousand people have managed it. Running a four-minute mile takes dedication, technique and tremendous effort; climbing

all the 8000m peaks requires all of the above but also carries a high risk of death.

Messner pushed the boundaries of stamina and determination as well as overcoming tragedy and setback to achieve success. He is a survivor and has inspired many mountaineers. He broke many psychological barriers during his mountaineering career, not least surviving many days in the death zone above 8000m.

As a young Alpinist I was influenced by his books, his climbing style and his ethics. He is an exponent of climbing fast and light and made daring rapid, solo ascents of big Alpine faces. He held a speed record on the North Face of the Eiger for some years, climbing it in ten hours with Peter Habeler in 1974. In the Himalaya he endured a traumatic descent on Nanga Parbat during which his brother Günther was killed; Reinhold survived the experience but with severe frostbite and had

all his toes amputated. Nevertheless he went on to climb all the 8000m peaks.

There is no doubt that Reinhold Messner is one of the world's greatest ever mountaineers. Distinctive looking, with a thick mane of hair, he is outspoken and has strong opinions on mountaineering and many other topics. I met him at the British Embassy in Kathmandu when he was a Euro MP for the Italian Green Party and we talked as much about European Politics as we did climbing.

Messner has a dedicated mountain museum in the Tyrol and is pretty much a household name in Europe. I have chatted with him at several mountain festivals in Britain and at Buckingham Palace, where we joined a gathering of fellow adventurers. It was salutary to realise that Messner, an Italian, was flattered and honoured to meet our Queen.

3 CHO OYU

8201M, 1990

Categorising any 8000m peak as 'easy', or referring to an 'ordinary' or 'normal' route to the summit, is a contradiction in terms. There is nothing easy or normal about any 8000m mountain. Each of the 14 giants represents a serious undertaking, with different characteristics, dangers, difficulties and local weather patterns, and none should be underestimated. However, Cho Oyu is generally regarded as the easiest and safest of the 14 and to safeguard the climb rope is fixed along the best route. It also has less avalanche and rock fall danger, fewer steep slopes and relatively easy access from Tibet.

Squat rather than pointy, Cho Oyu is a giant, snow-plastered whaleback, a huge Thunderbird 2 of a mountain but as impressive as any other 8000er, with a vast presence. Once fixed ropes are in place on the steeper sections it is a relatively straightforward ascent and the technical climbing difficulties are minimal. Unlike a lot of 8000ers there is no tricky, exposed final summit ridge to fall from – it has a large undulating summit plateau. The final section is like an extreme altitude fell walk to the summit. Cho Oyu attracts a number of teams every year and a well-marked route to the summit is created, making it a favourite for expeditions. It is a good first 8000er to attempt and is regularly guided.

Cho Oyu was to be the first of a double bill of two 8000m peaks in one season. We would climb Cho Oyu then go directly to Shisha Pangma, driving across the Tibetan Plateau. It almost felt as though we were using Cho Oyu to acclimatise. I was happy that we had gone to Cho Oyu first as I had already climbed Shisha Pangma. The original plan was to climb a new route on Cho Oyu and ensure all members of the L'Esprit d'Equipe climbing team reached the top together although I realised that our leader Benoit Chamoux would probably have an agenda to make sure of

Cho Oyu, sixth highest mountain in the world and possibly the easiest and safest 8000m peak... although there are no easy or safe 8000ers.

Inset photo

Benoit Chamoux and a friendly
Red Guard of the Chinese People's
Liberation Army in Tingri.

Left

Tingri, a stark and dusty village
at 4300m on the arid Tibetan
Plateau. Chinese development
has seen the village expand since
this photograph was taken in
1990. When I was last there coal
was being brought in by truck
from Chinese coal mines, to burn
on stoves instead of dried yak
dung. Coal gives a hotter and
cleaner fire than dung and the
increase in the village's population
means the yaks can no longer
keep pace with demand.

the summit himself, thus moving closer to completing all 14 of the 8000ers.

After a team launch in Paris, we flew to Kathmandu to organise the expedition kit before heading up the Friendship Highway north through Nepal to Tibet. Thankfully the road was free of landslides and we were able to drive all the way up to the Kodari Zhangmu border crossing and up to the Tibetan Plateau. I knew the road well by now, having been along it several times on expeditions to Tibet, such as Shisha Pangma with Jerzy Kukuczka and Menlungtse with Chris Bonington. To save time and money, as everyone had to pay a daily fee for each day they were in Tibet, Benoit insisted on pushing straight on to Tingri, high on the Tibetan Plateau at 4300m. Tingri is a dirty, bare, dusty, inhospitable mud-walled village. Imagine Clint Eastwood and the film *High Plains Drifter*, in brown and grey dust and yak dung. It's usually a good idea to stop for a few days in Nyalam, a thousand metres lower down, for the chance to acclimatise gradually and safely. Going too high too quickly causes serious acute mountain sickness (AMS) leading to cerebral and pulmonary oedema, which can rapidly be fatal.

I was not happy about going straight up to the Tibetan Plateau. On previous expeditions I had always had an acclimatisation stopover in Nyalam for two or three nights, which adds to expedition costs and time, but helps prevent AMS. Benoit often seemed like a man in a hurry, perhaps because he had to live up to his reputation as the fastest man to climb K2. I had experienced the effects of going too high too quickly before and it is very unpleasant. Pain sears through your head, which feels like it might explode, and lethargy sets in as though you have flu. All that speed was an unnecessary risk in my view. However, Benoit was the leader, he made the decisions and he insisted that we would be fine.

Just as I had feared, almost as soon as we reached Tingri I started to feel nauseous and unwell. I developed a pounding, burning headache, which would not go away. Paracetamol and aspirin had no effect. In the end, the team decided to put me in a Gamow bag, which was, at the time, a new piece of first aid equipment. Essentially, it is a big nylon coffin that acts as a mini-hyperbaric chamber. Pressure is built up within

A laden yak walks on ice at 4500m, carrying the ubiquitous blue barrels that keep equipment safe and dry.

in an attempt to fool the body into thinking it is a couple of thousand metres lower down. One of the Italians had also gone down with altitude sickness so we took it in turns to disappear inside the horrible bag. It didn't seem to do much for my splitting headache and I felt that the only cure was to descend to a lower altitude. A jeep to take the two of us to Zhangmu on the Nepal border would be expensive and taking two of us out of the expedition for three or four days would affect Benoit's plan for us all to summit together. Thankfully, Benoit started feeling the altitude badly too, so the three of us were driven down to benefit from the thicker air of Zhangmu. There, I immediately recovered. We spent a couple of nights at the much lower altitude, resting, drinking the odd bottle of Chinese beer, eating and gently exercising before driving back to Tingri, this time with another stopover, in Nyalam.

Altitude sickness is unpredictable. It can strike at any time and there seems no logical reason about who will get it and who will not. On this trip, Bull Computers had invested in an Inmarsat satellite telephone system so we could report our progress. These days, satellite communications are not much bigger than an ordinary mobile telephone but the system

we had for Cho Oyu involved several fridge-sized cases and a satellite dish as big as a large umbrella. The system was operated by a portly technician whose last physical exercise may well have been a PE lesson at school in the 1960s. Needless to say, he was the only one who remained relatively untroubled by altitude sickness throughout his stay at Base Camp, while all the super-fit mountaineers suffered.

Having lost time by descending to recover from AMS, we decided to adapt the expedition plan. The new route that we had hoped to try looked dangerously avalanche-prone as well as being a much longer approach from Base Camp. If we attempted it, no time would remain to climb Shisha Pangma before the monsoon arrived and as L'Esprit d'Equipe's plan was to climb two 8000ers back-to-back, we started up the so-called ordinary route.

Acclimatising well, with no more headaches I was having a wonderful time, in a masochistic kind of way. I was in my element, enjoying doing a lot of the lead climbing and fixing ropes as some of the lower sections involved steep pitches through icefalls. The climbing continued up and around seracs before easier-angled snow and ice slopes led to a final summit assault camp, at 7100m. The climbing was well within my technical capabilities and I could appreciate the expansive views across the Tibetan Plateau. We made rapid progress, working well as a team. Our training in France over the ten months since Manaslu seemed to have bonded us well.

I would have preferred the summit assault camp to have been higher than 7100m and to have been able to spend a bit more time acclimatising on the mountain before going to the top. I was not, however, making the decisions on this expedition and had to make a summit bid when it suited Benoit. It seemed slightly premature to me. The weather wasn't set fair enough and I would have been happier to put off the final push for a few days. As it was, most of us set off for the top individually at different times, depending on readiness. Benoit was keen to bag the summit before the weather broke. He set off while I stayed in the tent a few extra minutes to melt more snow to fill a water bottle.

Conditions were good initially, with a clear sky and firm snow, but the weather changed. Cloud seemed to curdle

Mealtime inside the L'Esprit d'Equipe mess tent at Cho Oyu Base Camp, at over 5000m. I am on the left in blue with a white headband. We are all wearing down clothing to protect against the bitter after-dark cold.

Left

Setting up the walkie-talkie relay mast above Base Camp in 1990, with Cho Oyu behind. The mast allows radio communication without the need for a line-of-sight signal between Base Camp and higher up the mountain. There is now a mobile phone network in the area and it's possible to make a call from the top of Cho Oyu or Everest.

round the summit slopes. A fairly gentle climb plugging steps up the snow slope led up to the rock band, where I had to scramble and wend my way up and around a couple of rocky sections before attaining the summit plateau. I remember having to force myself to concentrate as the climbing at that point involved scrambling and I needed to use my hands, not just plod up snow. It reminded me of the rock band on Pen-y-ghent in the Yorkshire Dales, or the Wainstones on the North York Moors.

Breaking through the rock barrier, I plodded steadily towards the summit, aware that I was moving slowly and steadily, alone in thick hill fog. A turbid layer of cloud enveloped the summit plateau but to me it felt like normal afternoon hill fog rather than a brewing storm. I did not

know where Benoit or the other climbers were. I was alone in the cloud. My pace was definitely slower than I would have liked and in the murky cloud I wondered whether I ought to turn back. But the fog seemed benign and I did not feel threatened or anxious by the conditions. I continued my solitary upward progress enveloped by dense, blanketing mist, determined to reach the summit.

The conditions were not as bad as I have experienced on many winter hills in the Scottish Highlands that are often shrouded by storm clouds and lashed by Atlantic or Arctic gales and I usually keep going through such weather. I had completed mountain training courses in such conditions, pushing on and navigating to a summit in poor visibility. For what seemed like hours I plodded through the greyish-white,

Opposite

Good weather and climbing conditions on Cho Oyu. On my ascent the summit was enveloped in cloud.

opaque world, slowly gaining height. I was concentrating on finding the highest point. The expansive, featureless, snow-covered summit of Cho Oyu is reminiscent of a Cairngorm hilltop, only bigger. It might as well have been an expanded Ben Macdui plateau, transported from Scotland in winter to Tibet, but without an Ordnance Survey trig pillar to mark the highest point. There was nothing on Cho Oyu to indicate the summit, no cross, statue, flag or pile of stones; I spent at least an hour and a half covering every inch of ground on the summit plateau until, in the end, I was absolutely certain that I could not get any higher. There was no more uphill. I was on the highest point at 8201m.

There was no view across to Everest, into Nepal or over Tibet. It was a semi-whiteout and visibility was only 20m, although occasionally the murk cleared to 50m or 100m. I did not bother to take any photos. There was nothing to see and I was more concerned with finding my way back before I became trapped in a full whiteout or deadly snowstorm.

There was still no sign of the rest of the team and there was no way I was going to wait on the summit for them in the sub-zero gloom. I had been wandering around in the cloud long enough. Body, mind and my mountain instinct were telling me that I needed to get to a lower altitude. I started to retrace my steps over the plateau and heard the muffled voices of the others in the mist. They were disorientated and daunted by the murky weather whereas I was well used to the thick hill fog affectionately known as clag in the British hills. When I reached them Benoit appeared through the mist and rounded everyone up for a team photo. We were all encased in hoods, goggles and mitts and in the thick cloud we could have been anywhere. It was good to be reunited and I felt relieved that everyone was safe. The others had no desire to wander around searching for the highest point and as the weather was not improving, a decision was made to descend. I was glad that I had pushed on alone to climb my third 8000m mountain.

My focus and concentration now were on finding the route back to and through the rock band and down to the high camp. Thankfully some bamboo wands, like golf course flags had been left to mark the route. The onward descent went smoothly and we rapidly returned to Base Camp. Cho Oyu had been an easy, uneventful ascent for me and I was now looking forward to another climb. After a short rest we drove across the Tibetan Plateau in 4x4s to Shisha Pangma Base Camp. As we were already acclimatised the team made a fast lightweight ascent of a new route on the north face, directly up a couloir to the right of the central summit 8013m. I now had two first ascents on that mountain; it seemed as if I was becoming an 8000m-peak aficionado.

SUMMIT FLAGS & FIONA

My personal summit flag has usually been a photograph of Fiona, my daughter. This little photographic print is like a paper talisman and thinking of Fiona gives me a nudge and reminds me not to be complacent on the descent and make sure that I safely return to Base Camp. I have been carrying a photo of Fiona as she's been growing up since she was one year old and over the years and many expeditions it has become like a mascot to me.

Many mountaineers carry their national flag to the summit of a Himalayan mountain. I am proud to be British and a Yorkshireman, but I have never felt the need to carry a Union Flag, Cross of St George or White Rose to a summit. I climb mountains for my own personal satisfaction, and even when I'm guiding

I get pleasure just from being on the hill. On Everest I had a photo of Fiona and my Gran, her Great Gran, who lived until she was a hundred. (There's hope for me yet.) On my last two 8000ers my photo was of Fiona and Jay, my grandson.

On the Gasherbrums in the Karakoram I accidentally left my summit photo in Islamabad and I wondered if that would be bad karma for me but I just had to carry on without it. On the summit of Gasherbrum I the British military team lent me their Union Flag for a summit photo. Now I can carry digital pictures and video clips on a camera or a mobile phone.

Often an expedition will have a national flag on a pole in Base Camp. I remember the Stars and Stripes flying at Gasherbrum I American Base Camp on the Upper Abruzzi

Glacier in Pakistan. At Kangchenjunga Base Camp I raised a Union Flag amid the Buddhist prayer flags, but I hoisted it upside down, which is a signal of distress. It certainly can be distressing in Base Camp and dangerous on the climb so perhaps it was apt.

Nepalese Sherpas always like to have garlands of Buddhist prayer flags around Base Camp and often take them to the summit along with a prayer scarf and sometimes a Nepalese flag.

I'm sure that having a picture of Fiona with me on my climbs contributed to my success, especially by keeping me focused and alert on the descent. It reminded me to survive, not just for my own selfish reasons, but also for better ones. After all, Fiona wanted her Dad back.

4 Broad Peak

8047m, 1991

Broad Peak is truly massive. The 12th highest peak in the world, its knife-edged, icy summit ridge is 1.5km long with sheer drops of 2500m on either side. Some people expect it to be easy because of its innocuous-sounding name, and because its slopes do appear to be gentle compared with peaks such as K2. Like any other 8000er, however, it is a serious undertaking and should not be underestimated. The first ascent was made in 1957, by an Austrian team including the legendary climbers Kurt Diemberger and Hermann Buhl, along with Fritz Wintersteller and leader Marcus Schmuck.

In late 1990 Bull Computers cancelled the funding for L'Esprit d'Equipe and the team was disbanded, although team leader Benoit Chamoux continued to invite me on expeditions until 1995, when he disappeared on Kangchenjunga. Offers of Himalayan climbs came my way from various people and, in 1991, shortly after returning from an attempt on Everest, I was invited as climbing leader and guide on a Broad Peak expedition. Luckily for me, Jagged Globe (then Himalayan Kingdoms) had done all the groundwork and planning, saving me the hassle of arranging the peak permit and finding sponsorship, so I could get straight on with it. It would be my first visit to the Karakoram and I could not wait to get up close to some of the spectacular giant mountains there.

Mountain guiding on an 8000m peak with a group of paying clients did, however, mean that my priority would be ensuring everyone's safety rather than bagging the mountain for myself. There were a dozen climbing clients and six trekkers who would go as far as Base Camp before returning home. That made quite a big team and for most Broad Peak would be their first experience of an 8000er.

Timing would be critical, as we had a fixed cut-off date and pre-booked flights home from Islamabad. We had to pull out by the deadline even if the summit had not been reached. The

Broad Peak seen from Concordia, the confluence of the Baltoro and Godwin Austen Glaciers, K2 at 8611m just appearing on the left. This was my first sighting of K2. The superlative view from here is more than worth the arduous ten-day trek in over moraine-covered ice along the Baltoro Glacier.

clients had to get back to their jobs and daily lives. We had been given about 60 days, which is tight for an 8000er. On a remote mountain such as Broad Peak it can take longer than two weeks to reach Base Camp and, in my experience, allowing at least 70 days for your expedition can make the difference between success and failure.

Landing in Islamabad was quite a culture shock. As Pakistan is an Islamic country you cannot just dive into a bar for a beer or two to get over the flight and start bonding with your team. Pepsi, Coke and Fanta are about the best you will get, unless you can inveigle your way into a High Commission or Embassy. Our local agent, Nazir Sabir, a well-known Pakistani climber who has become a great friend, welcomed us. Nazir had arranged the mountain permit with the Ministry of Tourism as well as arranging logistics such as Base Camp cooks and porters.

June in Islamabad is very hot and, after the required meetings with the ministry, we left the stifling heat and flew up country in a PIA 737 to Skardu. The spectacular flight was not for the faint-hearted, as the plane skimmed very close to the mountain ridges. Skardu, at 2500m in Baltistan, is the gateway to the Karakoram and the unpleasant effects of altitude can be felt as soon as you arrive. It is a dusty, ragged sort of place in a wide, grey-brown valley about 40km by 10km, near the confluence of the rivers Indus and Shigar. We ensconced ourselves in the K2 Motel compound, a basic, bare, uninspiring building surrounded by a high wall. It was like living within a small prison, although afternoon tea on the arid lawn, looking across the barren valley to the river, was pleasant enough.

A convoy of ramshackle jeeps took us from Skardu to Askole – the remote, mud brick village where the long trek with porters begins – along bumpy dirt tracks and exposed, precarious ledges hacked into cliff faces with sickeningly long drops.

One of the big differences in climbing in the Karakoram as opposed to the Himalaya is the remoteness of the mountains. We faced a difficult 12-day trek just to reach Broad Peak Base Camp, over the rough terrain of the Baltoro Glacier. In comparison, the walk-in to Everest from the Nepal side is less rugged, with villages, Sherpa lodges with showers and teashops lining the route.

We were a big group, 12 climbers with trekkers and Base Camp staff including cooks from Hunza in northern Pakistan. There must have been around 200 local Balti porters carrying our equipment and food to Base Camp, which was more like a scene from the 1950s. The porters were using makeshift rucksacks tied to their backs with what looked like bits of string and, although this looked uncomfortable, it did not seem to bother these hardy men. I was more used to seeing Nepali porters bearing loads in a *dhoko* – a traditional cone-shaped wicker basket – slung from their foreheads on a tumpline. One of the Hunza staff from Nazir's office in Islamabad was carrying a rucksack full of small denomination Pakistani rupee banknotes to pay the porter entourage. His load weighed 22kg and amounted to thousands of rupees. Also with us was a liaison officer, a captain in the Pakistan Army about to be promoted to major who was using the trek to gain high-altitude experience.

As a goodwill gesture after the first day's trek, a buffalo was slaughtered to help feed and keep the multitude of porters happy. It was a Halal killing, a rather gruesome sight to those unaccustomed to it, but the meat certainly got the porters in a good mood before the rigours of the Baltoro Glacier. Every morsel of the animal was shared out and eaten. Nothing but the blood went to waste.

Left
A Balti porter drinks murky water from a plastic bottle on the Baltoro Glacier, Karakoram. The locals in this part of Pakistan are not bothered about how silty and muddy the water is.

A steep gully section on Broad Peak.

We were not alone on the trek-in. The Pakistan Army was using the route to move supplies up to the Line of Control with India. Long lines of contractors' pack mules snaked over the glacier carrying food and munitions, and piles of dung were spread liberally everywhere, making it a problem to find clean water or ice to melt.

Views all along the Baltoro Glacier were spectacular, with dramatic mountains such as Trango, Masherbrum (K1) and Mustagh Tower rearing up on either side. The greatest masterpiece appeared after ten days when, from the remote glacier confluence known as Concordia, K2 appeared. Starkly proud, sheer and magnificent, with Broad Peak to its right, K2's dramatic presence filled the head of the Godwin Austen Glacier valley. I knew I would have to come back one day to climb it. All day long, on the trek from Concordia to Broad Peak Base Camp, K2 dominated the view ahead.

Once at the foot of Broad Peak, the trekking-only group set off for home. After the rest of us had established Base Camp, scraping flattish areas on the rubble-covered glacier ice, I needed to start checking the clients' skill levels. Nowadays, I would probably have met most of them before the trip and we would have trained together in Scottish winter conditions and in the Alps. It was interesting to realise that some had no idea how dangerous the climb would be, but all were fit and enthusiastic and we started acclimatising and setting up a string of camps on the mountain straight away. Everyone was climbing well and we were slowly moving camps higher up Broad Peak when the weather broke and a typical Karakoram storm engulfed the area, dumping half a metre of snow in Base Camp. After that, we were stuck there for more than a week, risking running out of time to make a summit bid. Climbing an 8000er is often a waiting game, pinned down in camp for many days, reading, listening to the BBC World Service, resting and eating.

Hanging around the camp was not keeping us fit so, one snowy day, I trekked up to K2 Base Camp. I had heard that there was a German expedition there led by Sigi Hupfauer, who had made the first winter ascent of the North Face of the Eiger and had climbed ten of the 8000m peaks. I regarded Sigi as a legend and was in awe of his

Setting off from the high camp at 7200m, heading to the col
at 7800m. The summit of Broad Peak is to the right.

achievements. He was very welcoming and we sat and had a brew while we chatted about K2 and his chances of getting to the top. I was surprised, flattered even, to realise that he had heard of me, as well as some of my first ascents and modest tally of three 8000ers.

When the weather cleared, I got back on the mountain with the clients and divided them into Teams A and B. Both teams were strong but it seemed Team A was most likely to summit, although no one can guarantee a summit; there are just too many variables in terms of weather, snow conditions and personal fitness. Suffering at altitude tends to be self-levelling for a lot of climbers and most soon realise that their aspirations will be limited by their tolerance of discomfort and risk as well as their capabilities. Inexperienced climbers and clients can overestimate their stamina and ability and often need to have their enthusiasm tempered. They often focus only on attaining the summit, forgetting that you must keep energy in reserve for the descent. Several times I have climbed to a summit with people who seemed full of energy and power, only to have them collapse on the descent. It seems to happen more with fit and strong, determined but inexperienced climbers.

By the third week, I had managed to get Team A to a high camp at about 7200m. We decided to make an attempt on the summit but the weather had other ideas. It closed in again and we had to retreat to Base Camp to recover. On the way down we met Team B coming up, and although Team A's members were exhausted, I felt strong and certainly able to have another attempt. Instead of returning to Base Camp for a rest, I transferred to Team B and headed back up the mountain. The weather started to clear and settle down. I felt that a calm window was developing and was keen to press on to the top camp and make a summit bid.

The final camp left just over 800m to ascend on the final push to the top. Initial snow slopes with some steeper

K2 from Broad Peak, with its classic ribbon of cirrus good-weather cloud. It usually forms about 800m below the summit.

Holding a photo of my daughter, Fiona, and my Grandma (Fiona's Great Gran) on the summit of Broad Peak, Pakistan, 16 July 1991. Behind me is Gasherbrum IV. I am kneeling on the edge of a precarious cornice with a 2500m drop into China below.

sections led gradually to the col at 7800m. From there a steep ridge reared up, impressive and certainly not a snow plod. I was looking after Ramon from Venezuela but he was starting to falter and I was concerned that he would burn out if he continued. I tried to reason with him and suggested turning back but he seemed somehow to gain extra strength and pushed on up. At 8000m the ridge to the summit eased off and became more level for the final kilometre to the highest point. For about an hour, it felt like we were walking along the roof of the world. On the left of the airy ridge was a 2500m-drop into China, on the right a similar plunge to the Godwin Austen Glacier in Pakistan. We plodded on slowly, gasping in the thin air. I was conscious that it was going to take the same time to trek back along that aerial tightrope before we could start descending.

When we reached the summit late in the day, at around 4pm, Ramon became the first Venezuelan to summit an 8000er. We hurried to snatch a few photos before turning back along the high exposed ridge and I now realised Ramon

was burnt out. His earlier exuberance and energy had drained. I had to force him to keep moving as he staggered with fatigue, hardly able to put one foot in front of the other. At times I was supporting him, his arm over my shoulder, as we shuffled painfully slowly along the roof-like summit ridge to the descent. Somehow he kept moving, along and down the steeper section of ridge to the col at 7800m where he gave up and collapsed in the snow. It was nearly dark, past 7pm, and the situation was becoming critical. Had I been alone, or abandoned Ramon, I could have been safely back down to the high camp by now, drinking tea. He muttered in broken English that he could go no further, that I should leave him there at the 7800m col and he reckoned he would follow on in the morning.

The light was fading fast and I told him he would die of exposure if I left him in the open overnight. I had absolutely no intention of spending a night out and getting frostbite. I knew that I had to get Ramon down. I could not leave him to certain death alone at this altitude. I gave him some of my water and chocolate, talking to him and trying to make him see the serious predicament he was in. I had to force him to care for his own life. After a long half-hour, as darkness was falling, I literally pulled him to his feet and we struggled on down. At times I half-carried him down the more easy-angled sections of the descent. It was nearly 11pm before we crawled into the haven of the little tent at 7200m. It had been an epic but luckily the weather had been kind and remained settled for the descent to Base Camp the next day.

Broad Peak was my fourth 8000er. I still had not set my sights on climbing all 14, which seemed an almost incomprehensible challenge. But I had seen K2, that towering, massive, challenging pillar of a mountain, and I was smitten.

CHAPATTI & CHIPS

The human body needs a massive amount of fuel – between 4000 and 5000 calories a day – to perform efficiently at altitude. Appetites often falter at altitude and such quantities are very difficult to eat and digest. You have to force yourself to eat, despite not feeling at all hungry.

I am often asked what I eat on expeditions and many people assume I rely on dehydrated meals. My usual answer is that I go on a 'seafood diet' – 'see food and eat it' – and my advice is to eat what you fancy. Just make sure that you get the calories and energy into your body.

In a base camp, at around 5000m to 5800m, my appetite is usually okay and I eat well. I used to avoid dehydrated food, which was not very appetising, although there are some good dried packet meals available now. Most people are accustomed to western processed foods and I used to ship food out from Britain – tinned fish and meat, chocolate and sweets, biscuits, cheese, drinks… anything I thought I might enjoy in a base camp or on the mountain – but latterly I've tried to source almost all my food in Kathmandu and in local villages on the trek to Base Camp. There is no need for tinned food; it is feasible to go native and to use fresh food just like the locals.

Variety is important. My expedition diets are primarily vegetarian because there is no beef in Hindu countries and no pork in Muslim countries. It is possible to get goat, sheep and chicken so I sometimes enjoy a chicken meal in Base Camp. You can also take eggs – nature's pre-packed food – and readily available fresh fruit including apples, oranges, small bananas – often about a third the size of those available in the UK – as well as pineapples and mangoes. If an expedition has sufficient budget, a porter could carry fresh food in every week, or for real extravagance a helicopter could drop supplies.

My Base Camp meals comprise primarily fresh local food such as *dhal bhat* (curried lentils with rice), curried boiled potatoes and chapattis. I also like fried eggs or omelettes with fresh chips and warm chapattis spread with Australian or Indian tinned butter.

On the climb above Base Camp, I used to take pre-packed food or 24-hour military ration packs. For my last few 8000ers, I switched to local foods such as hard boiled eggs, chapattis with jam and cheese, samosas, bhajis, mini cheese and onion pasties, chips and boiled potatoes, all pre-prepared in Base Camp and packed into plastic bags and supplemented with chocolate, tinned fish, energy bars and biscuits.

More important than food is fluid. Mostly on the climb snow and ice has to be melted for water, which is an arduous task at altitude when all you want to do is lie down and rest.

M y head ached and my body felt like it was being crushed in a vice. Climbing at extreme altitude is agony. Torture. Yet, even through that haze of suffering, my oxygen-starved brain was aware of the intense seriousness of my situation. No celebration was due yet. I was completely alone on the summit of K2, the world's second highest and possibly hardest mountain. Now I had to get down. Some of the world's best climbers have died descending K2. Many have been killed in good weather, with optimum conditions and in daylight. It was now between 6.30 and 7.00pm and the light was already fading. I would be descending in the dark.

I had to keep reminding myself, 'I must get down in one piece... No mountain is worth a life, or a finger or toe to frostbite... Returning from an expedition is a success. The summit is only a bonus.' I had to concentrate on the descent back to the world, back to my daughter Fiona.

As the sun dropped and the temperature plummeted even lower, K2 began to cast a huge triangular shadow across the Earth. The temperature was 40 below and in the bitter cold I realised frostbite was a real danger. I checked my headtorch and, drawing on many years of mountaineering experience, started my descent.

It was the culmination of three consecutive years' attempts on K2, known as the Savage Mountain. My first view of K2 had been from Concordia at the junction of the Baltoro and Godwin Austen Glaciers, on my way to Broad Peak four years earlier in 1991. Straddling the Pakistan–China border in the northern Karakoram, it pokes up dramatically from the barren rock-strewn glacier and moraine. At 8611m, K2 is a mountain of almost perfect proportions. Massive and impressive, it soars over 3000m in a stark pyramid of ice, snow and rock. To a mountaineer it is a glittering prize,

Looking up the Godwin Austen Glacier towards K2 from Concordia, Pakistan. The Abruzzi Spur (south east ridge) is on the right of the 3000m South Face; the Shoulder at 7900m to 8000m is above the wispy ribbon of cirrus. This cloud often forms around K2 and usually signifies good weather.

much more difficult than Everest. Although it is only 200m lower, it is steeper with more technical climbing, worse weather, avalanches, rock fall and a more arduous approach. Success on K2 equates to achieving the gold medal in mountaineering; Everest is the highest — but not really the first prize.

My first chance on K2 came in 1993 via the South East (Abruzzi) Spur on the Pakistan side. We were a lightweight team of four and made good progress acclimatising and pushing up the mountain. After three weeks, two of us were preparing for a summit bid and set out from a high bivouac at nearly 8000m. Two climbers from another expedition had gone to the top the previous day and we expected to meet them coming down as we went up. We came across only one. He was struggling to move, stumbling along a less steep section of the climb. I could see he was utterly exhausted and in danger of falling to his death down the 3000m South Face. His friend and climbing partner had already collapsed and fallen, gone, never to be found. It was a simple decision to abandon the ascent and rescue the stricken climber.

It took several days but we eventually managed to get him back to Base Camp. He survived but was badly frostbitten and had several toes amputated. The good weather window, which had offered hope of summit success, now slammed firmly shut for the season and with it went my opportunity to climb K2 that year. Before trekking out I explored the local area and chanced on the remains of the American Art Gilkey, lying on the glacier not far from Base Camp. He had disappeared 40 years earlier, probably in an avalanche down the Abruzzi Spur; we collected up the remains, took them out to Islamabad and passed them to the American Embassy.

A year later I made another attempt, this time with a US expedition to the North Face on the Chinese side. Very few people attempt K2 from the north — it is one of the most remote places on our planet. Even today, just getting to that part of the Karakoram is an adventure in itself and the whole expedition took nearly five months UK-to-UK. After an extraordinarily circuitous trip, involving several

Avalanche from the North Face of K2. It sent a huge cloud billowing into Base Camp, blasting the tents with snow; luckily most of its force had been spent.

flights through Tibet and China, we took jeeps through the Taklamakan Desert to the road head then trekked in with camels along the Shaksgam river valley to 3800m. From there we had three weeks hard graft, carrying all our loads to Base Camp at 5000m, as there were no porters or yaks to call on.

By June Base Camp was established and acclimatisation sorties on the mountain could begin. It was still bitterly cold, almost winter conditions, with green, wintry, iron-hard ice, brittle as glass. By July, conditions in the Karakoram are usually better, slightly milder although still sub-zero high up. Early on we had a ten-day spell of bad weather with Arctic blizzards trapping us in camp. Generally, however, the weather was better than usual and at times was too good, the heat of the sun in the clear sky melting out rocks and

causing serious stone fall, like incoming mortar fire. There were numerous avalanches so, although the weather was fair, conditions on the mountain were lethal. Nothing new there, then.

I had a close shave at 6000m, where I had dug a narrow ledge into the snow and ice slope for my small tent. Lying inside, on top of my sleeping bag, I heard the roar and felt the vibration of an approaching avalanche. Immediately I dived out of my tent and clung desperately to the rope fixed at the back of the ledge as a safety handrail. Simultaneously I tried to flatten myself against the ice wall as the avalanche poured over me like wet concrete. Its force was sucking me off the ledge and I was drowning under the wet mass. The tent was completely flattened beneath two metres of snow

Opposite

Two climbers follow me up the exposed, steep icy snowfield on the North Face of K2. This section of the climb is raked by stone fall and it reminded me of the ice fields on the North Face of the Eiger, which I had climbed many years before.

Left

On the North Face, at about 7800m, looking to the North K2 Glacier and Base Camp area 2500m below. Both lateral and medial moraines can clearly be seen on the glacier below. A textbook glacier.

and rock-hard ice blocks; I was lucky to be alive. Yet I was unable to move, buried thigh-deep in snow that had set like concrete. This was a bit serious, as I was clad only in my underpants. What an ignominious way to die, I thought, frozen to death in my Y-fronts. Luckily for me, two of my teammates on a nearby ledge were unharmed and were able to dig me out quickly, retrieving my boots and clothes from the tent before I suffered frostbite or hypothermia. In retrospect it was a serious incident and I was lucky to have survived although it was peculiarly funny.

In that far-flung corner of the world we believed we had the mountain to ourselves so we were surprised when a Spanish–Italian team turned up. They were a strong team and we were soon climbing together. On one sortie at around 6500m, one of the Spanish climbers pulled on some loose rock or an old rope and fell about 50m, tumbling down a sloping rocky section of the route. He stopped just above me, groaning and holding his arm, which seemed to be broken. As I went to his aid, one of his mates just ignored us and carried on up the mountain. I sat with him, and then helped him down to another of his teammates and they continued down to Base Camp together. His arm was splinted and he transferred to our expedition so that he could leave earlier with us while the rest of his team stayed on K2. By now, however, my team had had enough and my attempt for the summit would have to be made solo.

I spent another 11 nights alone, above 6800m, trying for the top. I was acclimatised and did not want to keep returning to Base Camp, although I was very aware that it was only a matter of time before I would start to deteriorate because of staying too high too long. The dangerous route traversed ice fields exposed to constant, deadly rock fall, similar to the North Face of the Eiger.

When I reached a tiny ledge at 8100m I let two Spanish climbers squash into my tiny tent with me. We would make a summit bid together. The final 500m is mostly an exposed hanging glacier of steep ice and snow clinging to the summit cone and is highly avalanche prone. I was apprehensive because it looked, and felt, very unstable. After climbing part of the way up and reaching a point only about five hours

Above

On the north ridge K2, looking out of the tent door at 7500m with a 2000m drop to the K2 Glacier. The Shaksgam Valley, China, is in the distance.

from the summit, with the weather looking clear and settled, I turned back. For me, the calculated risk was simply too high. The two Spaniards carried on. The slope did indeed avalanche. One died, the other survived but was badly frostbitten and had all his toes and fingers amputated.

My maxim has always been that no mountain is worth a life and yet, at the same time, I refused to let any such fatalities and stories of suffering put me off. Some people have accused me of being obsessed with K2, but I put it down to true Yorkshire grit. I was absolutely determined to get up it.

In 1995, after recovering from a serious leg injury on an aborted attempt at Makalu with Benoit Chamoux, I teamed up with British climber Alison Hargreaves and we set off together to join the 1995 American K2 expedition. Alison was an old friend and we had done a lot of climbing together in Britain. She had recently climbed Everest, while I had speared my leg en route to Makalu and spent time recovering in a Bangkok hospital. We flew from Islamabad to Skardu in a 737-passenger jet, an exciting and frightening trip, skimming low over the mountain ridges as it came in to land.

Right

The 'Eagle's Nest' 8000m, one of the few flattish places on the north ridge of K2. This is the final 'camp site', perched above a 2500m drop to Base Camp.

Relaxing with Alison Hargreaves on the trek in
to K2 Base Camp, Baltoro Glacier, Pakistan.

Alison and I trekked in for 12 days along the Baltoro Glacier to Concordia and the Godwin Austen Glacier leading to Base Camp. The American team, led by Rob Slater, was well established and theoretically three weeks better acclimatised than either Alison or me. There were a couple of other expeditions in camp, including a well-sponsored Dutch team. After a couple of weeks climbing with Alison, acclimatising and getting a feel for the conditions on the mountain, we changed partners. Alison teamed up with Rob and I started climbing with university professor and great character Richard Celsi.

I had now climbed four 8000m peaks. This was my 13th assault on an 8000er and my third consecutive attempt on K2, so I reckoned that I had enough experience. The Savage Mountain felt like an old friend, although I was starkly aware of the dangers it posed and knew that I must not get complacent and underestimate the risks on what was becoming familiar terrain. Despite the tightness in the scar on my recently wounded leg, I felt fit, acclimatised and ready for a summit push. My senses were telling me that the

The final hanging glacier at 8200m on K2's North Face. I was
climbing solo and turned back not far above this point. Two Spanish
climbers continued but later the slope avalanched. One was killed.
The other survived, but lost his toes and fingers to frostbite.

time was right. Conditions on the mountain seemed good, with a minimal avalanche threat.

A good weather window was opening and I knew I had to go for it. Richard had to retreat but I pushed on alone solo to the shoulder at 8000m, where so many had died in the 1986 K2 disaster, including British climbers Alan Rouse and Julie Tullis. I was well aware that if the weather deteriorated I could become trapped here at 8000m and quickly perish. The frisson of real danger seemed to keep my mind crystal clear. I knew that I had to seize the opportunity in the benign conditions and grab the big prize – K2's summit.

The shoulder has a flattish, snow-covered area, into which I dug a grave-like trench for my tiny bivouac tent. At 8000m I was well and truly in the death zone; all I could do was melt snow for water to keep hydrated and conserve energy for an enormous effort the following day. It could be a ten-hour climb to the top and another three to five hours back down, so I planned to set off before dawn, at around 2am. As I prepared alone for my summit push, a four-man team from the Dutch expedition turned up, two Dutch along with two Pakistani climbers.

In the early hours of 17 July it was close to 3am by the time I had warmed my boots and started to function, setting off in the rarefied, gin-clear, painfully cold air. All four of us co-operated and fixed thin 6mm Kevlar rope in the steep icy couloir known as the Bottleneck – a spooky, perilous gully overhung by a hideous serac of glistening blue-white ice which towers like a malevolent Beachy Head or White Cliffs of Dover. Massive lumps of ice regularly calve and crash down, obliterating anything below. I was relieved to climb out of the line of fire and begin a diagonal leftwards traverse on to the summit slopes. A series of steep ice bulges and icy steps eventually led to a final airy snow ridge with a sensational 3000m drop directly to Base Camp.

By now it was nearly 6pm. I had been struggling up for more than 15 hours, taking huge risks. It would soon be dark. On the summit I managed to pass my camera to one of the Dutch climbers for a photo of myself with my picture of Fiona before the others left without a word, not even so much as a warning to remind me to get a move on.

Above

Climbers in murky afternoon cloud at 6500m on the Abruzzi Spur.

However, I was glad. I was alone. I had the summit of K2 to myself while its stupendous looming shadow, cast in the setting sun, stretched to and above the horizon. Usually it is best to spend only a few minutes on a summit such as K2's. Linger too long at extreme altitude and you will die. I must have been there at least 45 minutes, perhaps nearly an hour, filming and generally trying to appreciate the most inhospitable spot on the planet. At one point I remember feeling a dream-like sensation, that the summit was gooey porridge and I was stuck in it, anchored to the top. Pulling myself out of the ominous reverie I focused on the task in hand – getting down, surviving K2.

As nightfall enveloped me, I tore myself away from the summit and summoning up deep reserves of stamina and energy, began the steep descent. Fortunately I am pretty confident, efficient and fast on descents, while still taking every care to be safe. I quickly overtook the other four, who were going slowly, and reached the relative safety of my bivouac on the Shoulder at around 10pm. Exhausted, I crawled inside to rest. Alone in my tent at 8000m in the death zone darkness, I said 'Thank You' out loud to some unspecified greater presence.

Opposite

Leaving Camp 1 (6450m) on the Abruzzi Spur, the south east ridge of K2.

With a picture of my daughter Fiona on the summit of K2 17 July 1995. After this photo was taken I was alone on the summit filming and trying to appreciate the achievement. I spent too long up there, nearly an hour, before I solo climbed back down to the Shoulder.

If the weather broke, I knew I would almost certainly be trapped and die, as had happened to those unfortunate souls in 1986. Somehow I felt the weather would hold fair until morning and decided to wait rather than push on. I had a hunch that all was going to be okay and that I would make it safely down. But no ascent is complete, and no success can be tallied until you have safely returned to Base Camp. Alertness and concentration on the descent are essential for survival.

I met Alison and Rob at about 6000m. They congratulated me but then Alison burst into tears from the sheer frustration of missing her chance. The summit was now engulfed in a massive lenticular cloud. The clear weather window had slammed shut.

I could have hung around Base Camp, where other climbers waited and hoped for another good spell of weather, but for me K2 was done. I had spent nearly 11 months over three years tangling and tussling with the turbulent peak and was ready for home. Unusually, the monsoon had pushed up into northern Pakistan and K2 was being battered by storms. Even my trek out was eventful with landslides, mudflows, rock falls, blocked roads and washed away bridges in what was the worst monsoon since the founding of the state of Pakistan.

A week or so after returning to Britain from K2, the news broke that Alison and Rob were among the climbers who had perished in a brutal storm high on K2. Only five climbed K2 that year; eight died there. It truly is the Savage Mountain.

THE DEATH ZONE

The region above 8000m (realistically above 7500m) is the most inhospitable on the planet. It is impossible for human beings to survive there for more than a few days at the most, no matter how well-acclimatised they are. Life expectancy can be measured in hours. The oxygen-depleted air is too thin, the atmospheric pressure too low. It is known as the death zone.

Being at extreme altitude is unpleasant and dangerous, and an ability to overcome suffering and tolerate hardship is essential. Symptoms of mountain sickness – a bodily malaise, nausea, headaches, shortness of breath or gasping and a rapid pulse rate – can be felt at much lower altitudes and care needs to be taken even well below 8000m. Acute mountain sickness (AMS) can rapidly develop into either high altitude pulmonary oedema (HAPE) or high altitude cerebral oedema (HACE), both of which are killers.

The environment within the death zone is extremely hostile and harsh. All the water you need for survival is locked in snow and ice and requires great effort to melt. The sub-zero temperatures increase the risk of frostbite, exacerbated by dehydration from inhaling dry, cold air as you breathe. Levels of ultra violet light are high so areas of exposed skin – even the inside of your mouth, your tongue and your gums as you gasp in the rarefied atmosphere – are at risk of burning.

There is very little anyone can do to help or rescue someone from within the death zone. It is my belief that you would stand more chance of being rescued if you were on the Moon, or orbiting Earth aboard the International Space Station; at least the technology exists to enable something to be done. The death zone, however, is too high for helicopters, for which the landing and operating ceiling is around 6500m, and there are no mountain rescue teams. Even if there were, it would take them a couple of weeks to acclimatise.

In the death zone, you are on your own.

K2 north side sunset. 'The Savage Mountain'. Five months away from home, but I turned back high on the snowfield at the top because of the high avalanche risk.

6 EVEREST

8848M, 1996

Rongbuk 5200m. This is the road head and Base Camp on the north side of Everest in Tibet. Mallory and Irvine camped here in the 1920s, when it was the traditional site of British Base Camps, and I helped to cement in a memorial plaque to them in 1996. The Chinese have built concrete toilet blocks and an interpreter and liaison officer building here. Many trekkers and tourists can now reach this spot by bus. A hotel has been built nearby and mobile phone masts erected. The top of the moraine mound on the right has also since been levelled off to create a tourist viewing point. I watched a digger lumber up to excavate the mound in April 2011.

For several minutes on 19 May 1996, no one on the planet was higher than me. I stood on the summit of Everest, the top of the world, as high it is possible for a human being to climb. Yet I felt a strange anti-climax. It was as if I knew the view, as if I came up here every month. I could almost have been on Mont Blanc, Ben Nevis, Helvellyn or even my familiar local hill Roseberry Topping in North Yorkshire, rather than the highest mountain on Earth. I remember thinking that I should feel overwhelmed and bursting with emotion, or cry. I didn't. I just got on with the job of filming and taking photographs, the professional cameraman and photographer in me clicking into work mode.

The view from the summit was exceptional. It seemed as if I could see the curvature of the Earth – to the north over the barren, brown plateau of Tibet and to the south the lush valleys of Nepal. I had climbed the North Ridge of Everest from Tibet and I looked down the South East Ridge, towards the South Summit, the South Col and Nepal. There were no tracks at all, so no one had been up from the Khumbu Region for a while. Not far down, there was a bare patch of exposed rock and I wondered whether that was the Hillary Step. Beyond I could see Lhotse, at 8516m the world's fourth highest mountain, the steep gully line of its ascent route clearly visible. I made a mental note for next year. That distinct almost vertical couloir cutting through the west face was the route I intended to climb.

The final highest snow cone on Everest is about the size of two king-size beds, enough room to relax if it were a few thousand metres lower. There was a cluster of poles and what looked like plastic lights on top, probably left from some laser or GPS surveying. All was festooned with prayer flags and ceremonial silk scarves, fluttering in the wind like ragged dirty washing.

Buddhist prayer flags adorn the desolate Pang La 5200m. This high pass en route to Everest Base Camp has superlative views to Everest and Cho Oyu. The classic banner cloud can be seen streaming from the summit of Everest. This phenomenon is often referred to as Everest 'smoking' like a steam locomotive or a steam ship at sea.

I wanted to enjoy my moment on top of the world, to savour the feeling, but strangely, I did not feel the tingle of fear and seriousness that I had experienced on K2's summit ten months earlier. Everest felt tame. I was confident of getting down although I knew I mustn't be complacent. Eight climbers had been killed only nine days ago in a ferocious storm. Three bodies were still frozen to the slopes on the North Ridge above 8300m and I had passed close to them on my way up. Their bodies reminded me of my mortality, that it could easily happen to me, too, but there was nothing I could do to recover them. It would take a protracted effort by a strong team of six or eight people to move a body, a very risky undertaking above 8000m.

All too soon I had to leave the top of Everest and concentrate on the descent. The top of the North Ridge route is dramatically exposed, with a 3000m drop down the Kangshung Face on one side and a 2500m plummet to the Rongbuk Glacier on the other. Before I left the summit I spoke to Base Camp on the radio. Actor and fellow Yorkshireman Brian Blessed was resting there after we had made an earlier summit attempt together, which had almost succeeded. I had carried his Buddhist prayer scarf, blessed by the Dalai Lama, to the summit for him.

'Alan to Base. Alan to Base. I'm on the summit. Are you there Brian? Over,' I yelled into the radio.

'Well done Alan! I love you! Well done! Congratulations! Can you see me? I'm waving! I can see you, my boy! I love you! Well done my boy! I love you! I'm waving! I love you! Over.'

'Yes I can see you, Brian,' I bantered back, although I couldn't even see Base Camp at that distance, any more

The broad snowy North Ridge and North East (skyline) Ridge of Everest, from the North Col at 7000m. Climbers are visible on the North Ridge and you can see the whole of the route Mallory and Irvine took. Note the First, Second and Third Steps and the summit pyramid, as well as the pinnacles (at the top of the North East Ridge) where Pete Boardman and Joe Tasker disappeared in 1982.

Loose shaley rock on the North Ridge 7600m, looking down to tents on the North Col 7000m. The slope in shadow to the right leads down to Advance Base Camp 6400m and the East Rongbuk Glacier.

than he could really see me. 'Your scarf is fluttering in the jet stream,' I said, although if it had really been the jet stream I would have been torn off the summit by the roaring wind. But his scarf was flapping in a strengthening breeze so I realised that I should think about setting off back down.

Brian's Shakespearean voice continued: 'Wish I could be up there with you Alan. I'm with you in spirit, mate. Love you. Come back down safely. There's a big hug waiting. Well done. Love you! Over!' As well as being a great actor, Brian is truly a larger-than-life character.

As the cloud started to swirl around Everest's summit I began my descent, spurred on by the anticipation of a big hug from Brian. It was a day-and-a-half before I reached the spartan, windswept Advanced Base Camp on the East Rongbuk Glacier at 6400m, just below the North Col. It's a desolate place, set on the creaking, groaning ice where the glacier inexorably but almost imperceptibly moves down the valley. After a day's rest I trekked down to the more salubrious surroundings of the Rongbuk 5200m Base Camp, road head and a welcome bottle of Chinese beer.

My first visit to the Big E, as Everest is affectionately known, had been to the north side in 1984. Travelling through China in the early 1980s was an incredible experience, with everyone – millions of people – dressed in the same blue or green Mao suits. There were few cars and the roads were flowing rivers of bicycles. Without the noise of traffic, the cities seemed surreally quiet. Nowhere felt threatening and the Chinese were very welcoming and friendly. Tibet was just starting to be developed and transport to Base Camp, across the desolate arid Tibetan plateau, was in open-backed military trucks. It was a horrible, freezing cold, gritty affair on rough dirt roads and we had to wear high-altitude suits and face masks to combat the bitter cold and dust.

It was pretty quiet at Base Camp in those days and we had the mountain to ourselves. I made a solo push above 7100m, heading up the Central Couloir on the North Face. Although I was fit and raring to go, it was not to be. An enormous avalanche, of a size that generally occurs only every quarter-century, crashed into Advance Base Camp,

killing one climber and seriously injuring a number of others. The next week was spent rescuing and evacuating the injured to the road head. The dead climber was buried in a crevasse on the mountain. Finally, the leader of our expedition had a heart attack at 6500m, entailing another protracted rescue. Fortunately he survived and we got him back to Britain for surgery. It was an eventful expedition during which I learned much about extreme altitude, not least the immense danger from cold, wind, lack of oxygen and avalanche as well as essential skills such as conserving energy and moving at a steady pace. That was when I realised that mere survival is a success.

My next attempt on Everest was in 1991 and this time we flew directly to Lhasa from Kathmandu before travelling overland to Base Camp. By then many more Chinese buildings had sprung up in Tibet, the roads had been improved and a few other expeditions were at Base Camp, attempting Everest. I was climbing with my American friend Steve Untch, with whom I'd climbed Shisha Pangma. It was good to be reunited. We made a good team and were on the same wavelength, sharing a similar sense of humour and an ability to suffer. However, the expedition we were part of pulled out to go home too early, leaving Base Camp on 25 May. As we left Base Camp to go down, the weather was perfect for a summit push. It was very frustrating for Steve and me. The first ascent of Everest in 1953 had not been until 29 May, so I could not understand our early departure. The weather settles down at the end of May and, even into early June, it is possible to climb on the north side from Tibet. It can be very frustrating to have a fixed cut-off date for an expedition. If you really want to climb an 8000m peak you need to be committed to stay as long as it takes.

I put Everest on the back burner after that attempt and there it remained, almost forgotten, for a few years. It might be the highest but Everest is not the necessarily the greatest mountaineering challenge. Instead my attention focused on K2 for four years. When I eventually climbed K2 in 1995, I filmed on the very summit, proving that I could shoot in the most inhospitable, dangerous places. As a result, I was invited to film Brian Blessed on his Everest climb the following year and my remit was to get to the top and film, which suited me.

On that 1996 climb all my expenses were covered. It was a well-organised expedition and, as a cameraman, I was being paid a small fee. Although I had climbed K2, which many mountaineers class as the first prize, I really did want to climb Everest and stand on top of the highest mountain in the world.

Once again I was attempting the mountain from Tibet, following in the footsteps of Mallory and Irvine. We took a memorial plaque to the 5200m Base Camp where they had camped in 1924. It was cemented into a cairn on a moraine mound within sight of the summit of Everest and the North Ridge, on which they were last seen going for the summit. Although my job was cameraman, as a mountain guide I ended up helping some of the other team members, including Brian.

Reaching Base Camp was now even more straightforward. You could drive to 5200m in a minibus along a mixture of tarmac, concrete and well graded and maintained dirt roads. Big clouds of opaque dust and dirt would billow up behind the vehicles and fine particles of grit would penetrate your every pore. It was a good idea to wear a face mask to protect your lungs. Worse, grit would penetrate cameras, clog up mechanisms and scratch lenses.

Getting to Base Camp healthy and with cameras that worked was the first challenge. Once there, the second was preventing the Tibetan locals and yak herders from stealing our equipment. We employed Sherpas from Nepal, who helped guard our Base Camp area to deter thieves during the night. Even the higher camps had to be guarded.

Climbing Everest from the north offers a different experience from the Khumbu region of Nepal to the south. The Tibetan side is barren, windswept and rocky. Generally it is a steeper proposition, with more bare rock, less threat from seracs and avalanches but more exposure to the wind, which often made the climbing colder. There is no dangerous Khumbu Icefall to climb through. You trek up

to 6500m with yaks carrying supplies for an advanced base camp. From there you climb straight up steep snow and ice to the North Col at 7000m. Although not as dangerous as the Khumbu Icefall, many climbers have been avalanched and killed on the 500m slope. From the North Col the route climbs steadily up a broad, often windswept ridge, to join the narrower north east ridge.

Higher up the main technical difficulties are the First and Second Steps. Climbing ropes are fixed along much of the route, to safeguard ascents and descents. On the Second Step, at around 8600m, a short section of alloy ladder – the sort you might buy in a British DIY store – has been secured to the rock. It was the Second Step where Noel Odell last saw Mallory and Irvine in 1924 'going strongly for the top'. To this day, the question of whether they could have made the summit is surrounded by mystery and debate. Could they have climbed the vertical Second Step at 8600m? I wonder whether we will ever know for sure. I was looking forward to climbing those historic, significant steps, steeped in the history of the earliest attempts on Everest in the 1920s and 1930s.

Climbers near the First Step 8500m. It is still nearly 400m to the top of Everest from here. Cloud condenses and billows up the 3000m Kangshung Face. Seen from a distance Everest will be 'smoking' with its trademark banner cloud streaming from the summit ridge. The hills of Tibet can be seen in the distance.

Since I first visited the Rongbuk in 1984 the area had developed. The Buddhist monastery had been rebuilt in a smaller format and monks were living there. The hardcore road was better graded and there was a concrete blockhouse for Chinese and Tibetan interpreters and liaison officers. There was also a concrete long-drop toilet building at the road-head Base Camp at 5200m. The latter was not a pleasant place to visit as a two-metre stalagmite of

Below

Vertical climbing at the Second Step 8600m is exhausting at this extreme altitude. I climbed it too quickly and at the top nearly blacked out with the effort. A Chinese expedition fixed part of this vertical wall with a ladder, which has since been replaced with a larger ladder. The grey alloy ladder looks like it has come from a DIY store. Could Mallory and Irvine have climbed this obstacle in 1924, or did they avoid it by skirting round under it on exposed ledges?

excrement would build up in the sub-zero temperatures and from time-to-time would need poking down with a big stick.

Today, the area is being managed and kept relatively clean, with rubbish collection points and better toilet sites but conditions at Base Camp in 1996 certainly spurred us all on to our sorties onto the mountain.

Everest is a honey pot and will always attract climbers and would-be climbers who want to stand on top of the world. Nowadays the climbing might be less technical, with ropes fixed to help progress up and down, but it is still a worthwhile climb and the dangers of avalanche, extreme weather, frostbite and extreme altitude remain. Even though today you can buy your place on an organised, sometimes guided, expedition, Everest should not be underestimated – its ascent is still a deadly challenge.

Right

The Mallory and Irvine memorial
at Rongbuk 5200m, with the
snout of the Rongbuk Glacier
just visible behind. Mallory and
Irvine disappeared high on the
north side of Everest in 1924.

Opposite

Looking to the summit of Everest 8848m from 7700m
on the North Ridge. The last photograph of Mallory
and Irvine was taken near here by Noel Odell on
8 June 1924. Odell commented that he saw them
'going strongly for the top'. The First Step is the
pimple on the ridge in the centre of the photo. The
Second Step is the next vertical step, followed by
the Third Step and final snowy summit pyramid.

MALLORY & IRVINE

On 8 June 1924, George Mallory and Andrew Irvine were last seen on the North East Ridge of Everest 'going strongly for the top', according to fellow climber and observer Noel Odell. Mystery has long enshrouded the question of whether they reached the summit before perishing on the descent or came to grief while still ascending.

Professor Odell was a geologist, accustomed to making observations and giving accurate descriptions of terrain. He was convinced that he had seen two figures climb the Second Step before disappearing into cloud. Like many people, I would like to think that they did reach the summit in 1924, nearly 30 years before Edmund Hillary and Tenzing Norgay. Even if they did, however, my view is that the credit for

the first ascent – and more importantly the safe return to Base Camp – cannot be taken away from Hillary and Tenzing.

I climbed the North East Ridge, including the First and Second Steps, in 1996. The Second Step is a steep face, at around 8600m. Depending on snow build-up, it comprises a 25–30m rock wall with a 5m vertical face at the top. A wide crack in its left corner creates an open book-like feature, which I overcame with the help of a rickety alloy ladder, loosely tied to the right wall. I remember perhaps climbing too quickly and collapsing above it for several minutes, gasping for air, my pulse racing. I had made a point of examining the crack and thought it might be possible to climb, whereas the wall behind the ladder seemed smoother and less climbable. The technical grade of

the crack looked about British VS. If you were well acclimatised and had warmer weather – as Mallory and Irvine had in June 1924 – it might be possible. Mallory was a talented rock climber and it would have been comfortably within his capabilities at a lower altitude. A bigger problem would be descending the rock step when returning, exhausted, from the summit.

Odell thought that he had observed two figures climbing the Second Step at the base of the final pyramid. Could that actually have been what is now known as the Third Step? Perhaps they had already avoided the difficult Second Step by traversing beneath it on snow as some climbers have done since, to reach the Third Step. If so, as Odell put the time at about 1pm, it is quite possible they reached the summit that afternoon.

Mallory intended to leave a photograph of his wife on the summit and, when his body was found in 1999, no photograph was recovered. Could he have reached the top and left it there? Unless a camera is found with a salvageable summit photograph, we might never know.

Moonrise over the North West Face, seen from high on the slopes of Gasherbrum II.

7 GASHERBRUM I

8068M, 1996

My personal challenge was to solo climb two 8000m peaks back-to-back, on one expedition. Gasherbrum I, sometimes known as Hidden Peak, was to be the first, followed by Gasherbrum II.

I now had considerable 8000m peak experience; this would be my 15th expedition to extreme altitude. As well as being more dangerous I knew that climbing an 8000er solo would also be a test of my psychological resilience as well as my physiological strength, stamina, skill and determination.

Everest did not seem to have debilitated me much, even though 1996 had been a tragic season with a major storm and a lot of deaths. There was no time to reflect on my achievement or to bask in the publicity aftermath. After a few days back in the UK to wash my clothes, see my daughter Fiona and have a beer with a few mates, I left again for Pakistan.

In the space of ten months I had climbed and survived unscathed the two highest mountains on the planet, K2 and Everest. I now intended to climb two more 8000m peaks before the 12 months were up. Four 8000m peaks in a year would give me a total of eight out of the 14, more than half way to the Grand Slam. I was even beginning to consider climbing all 14.

I had organised the expedition to Gasherbrum I and II before departing for Everest, and had arranged a permit for both with my Islamabad-based Pakistani trekking and climbing agent. I intended to climb them back-to-back because they are close together and use the same base camp, in a remote part of Kashmir, not far from the India–Pakistan border known as the Line of Control. The base camp is a longer trek in and the area even more desolate and isolated than K2 Base Camp.

To help cut costs I intended to share the expense of the mountain permit, dining tent, cook, sirdar and trek-in porters with three other climbers from Germany and Austria. Once I left Base Camp I would be on my own, solo climbing. There would be no team to back me up and no porters on the mountain to fix tents or help carry loads. My tentative plan was to move fast and light, Alpine-style, climbing Gasherbrum I first before moving directly to Gasherbrum II without returning to Base Camp. Very few climbers have ascended two 8000m peaks back-to-back. It is debilitating and needs luck with a good weather spell. In 1987 I went directly from Shisha Pangma to Lhotse South Face, then again in 1990 from Cho Oyu to Shisha Pangma. Even now, I had only been back in Britain for a few days after Everest and I was heading out to another 8000er.

My fifth visit to Islamabad was a good opportunity to catch up, albeit briefly, with Pakistani and ex-pat friends based at the High Commission. June is mango season but I didn't linger long to savour them before heading up the Karakoram Highway to the road head at Askole.

The Baltoro trek-in was becoming a familiar route for me, but this time I shared the walk to Gasherbrum I with an Austrian couple and a German dentist. Thoughts of the film *Marathon Man*, which starred Laurence Olivier and Dustin Hoffman, came to mind, especially when, ironically, one of my fillings came out. In the film, the German dentist (Olivier) tortures Marathon Man (Hoffman) by drilling a tooth. When I mentioned the film clip to the German dentist he told me he had seen it but that I did not have to worry and he kindly and sensitively stuffed some temporary filling compound into the hole in my tooth.

The walk-in was long and arduous but, as it was the fourth time I had trekked up the Baltoro, I knew what to expect. I settled into the 12-day yomp, passing now-familiar mountains and campsites. Oddly, the Austrian couple wanted me to race them each day to see who could

The snout of the 62km-long Baltoro Glacier, Karakoram, Pakistan, looking towards the Trango Towers. This is one of the longest glaciers outside the polar regions and source of the Braldu river.

Glacier. We continued up the Gasherbrum Glacier for another two days. Artillery shells fired from the Indian side of the border had supposedly landed in the area during periods when Pakistani troops had been trying to advance to the Indian side of the Line of Control or threatening to attack Indian positions. Some of the military observation posts were at 6000m or higher, on ridges or other high inhospitable points in this part of the Karakoram.

We reached Base Camp to find a British Joint Services Expedition already installed, as well as a Spanish team. These Joint Services Expeditions are organised about every four years. There were a few old friends in the camp, which meant I was never lonely. In fact I was welcomed almost as an honorary team member and often joined them for meals. They had a good stock of books to supplement those I had brought along. Someone recommended *Complicity* by Iain Banks. I could feel and smell Scotland in the story and was whisked away to Edinburgh, the Forth Road Bridge and the A9. I have been a fan of Iain Banks ever since.

Later I teamed up with a couple of the lads to ascend through the crevassed area of the glacier that leads up to the steeper climbing above Base Camp. That made it a lot safer for me, especially when crossing unstable snow bridges spanning crevasses. If one of those bridges had collapsed when I was unroped and climbing solo, I would have fallen many metres into the crevasse with no chance of survival or rescue. The opportunity to negotiate the heavily-crevassed glacier above Base Camp safely with a couple of competent and fun Brits was a bonus.

Normally, I would try to get in three good weeks of acclimatisation before making a summit bid. Now, after the trek in and a couple of nights in Base Camp, I was raring to go. The Brits were amazed at first and possibly slightly envious when, after only a couple of days' rest, I was able to set off on a summit attempt. I had to remind them that I had only recently been acclimatising on Everest.

I reckoned it would increase my chances if I went for the top at the same time as the British military team. They were happy for me to join them as it would help with route finding and trail breaking. Psychologically, although I would

Left

South West Face of Gasherbrum I 8068m (Hidden Peak). This 2000m face dominates the view from Base Camp on the upper Abruzzi Glacier.

reach the evening campsite first. That is not a good recipe for acclimatisation. It is better to pace yourself, ascend gradually, avoid stress and try to enjoy the journey. So I ignored them. They even taunted that I was too slow and unfit to climb an 8000er. I was bemused by their bizarre behaviour and wondered what they were trying to prove but I just got on with the climb. In the end, they failed to climb Gasherbrum I and returned to Austria earlier than planned.

The glacier junction of Concordia is where those heading for Broad Peak and K2 turn left up the Godwin Austen

Opposite

On the South Gasherbrum Glacier at 6200m. The icefall leads up to the hidden Upper Gasherbrum basin. Two climbers can be seen on the flat glacier just left of centre, dwarfed by the scale of the surrounding mountains and Karakoram's glacial terrain.

British Joint Services Expedition tents perched on an exposed bivouac site at about 7200m on the shoulder of Gasherbrum I. My small bivi tent was also placed here for my solo climb to the top. In the end I was not alone but had the pleasure of the company of four great chaps from the Joint Services Expedition on my climb. Masherbrum (K1), can be seen in the distance.

be solo climbing, I would feel less vulnerable having fellow Brits around. It was going to be much more fun, if climbing an 8000er can ever be described as 'fun'.

I was quietly confident but still cautious as, with a couple of the British Services climbers, I moved up to a high camp at 6500m below the steep 1500m climb to the top. We spent an entire afternoon on the col between Gasherbrum I and Gasherbrum II, melting snow on stoves for 'wets' as the lads call drinks and enjoying the unusually good weather.

From there the route became a steep snow and ice slope, with a couple of rocky steps in a broad gully, known as the Japanese Couloir. Technically, it was about Winter Grade 2 to 3 and pretty difficult to solo climb at this altitude. Near the top, the gully narrows as you break out onto a shoulder at over 7100m.

Here I had to dig into the slope to make a ledge for my tiny one-man bivouac shelter. It took me more than an hour to scrape out an area flat enough to balance my tent on before I could attempt to lie down on the sloping ledge and get my stove out to melt snow. Four of the Brits were on the shoulder with me, as well as some of the Spanish climbers, all taking advantage of the fair weather.

Next day four Brits, several Spaniards and myself headed off pre-dawn, about 1am, using head torches. The final 800m of ascent was mostly on steep snow and ice. We took it in turns to lead climb and break trail. There were sections of deep snow and I would have found it very slow and much harder if I had been alone with no one to help plug steps. In the end it was a great team effort.

On the summit I handed my camera to one of the lads for a summit photo. There were amazing views to Gasherbrums II, III, IV, Broad Peak and K2. Gazing across to Gasherbrum II, my next objective, I studied the route up the ridge and face to the top and hoped the weather would hold so I could bag it without returning to Base Camp. We had a group photo on the summit and shook hands but I was not able to hold up a picture of my daughter Fiona for the shot as I usually did. I had somehow left it back in Islamabad and remember feeling at the time that it might be bad karma. One of the Brits had a Union Flag, so instead I

On the summit of Gasherbrum I,
10 July 1996, with Gasherbrum II,
Broad Peak and K2 behind. I have
borrowed the Union Flag from
the British military lads. The
cardboard film box taped to my
sunglasses is unsightly, but doing
a good job as a nose protector
to prevent sunburn from the
intense high-altitude UV light.

had a photo taken with that. It was great to be on top with such a good bunch of lads.

So far Gasherbrum I had gone smoothly and the weather even looked set fair. I tried not to think about Gasherbrum II and instead concentrated on getting down in one piece. In the back of my mind I could not help thinking I might get Gasherbrum II done, then walk out with the Brits.

I set off down well ahead of the others. I can usually descend faster than other climbers. Even on steep snow slopes I face out and move fast, sometimes running down when others are facing in and moving down slowly. There is no doubt that facing the slope to descend slowly and methodically is safer but getting down and out of danger as fast as possible is my favoured approach, especially on 8000ers.

Suddenly I heard shouts. I looked back and saw a body sliding at breakneck speed down the slope from near the summit. The figure started cartwheeling, accelerating and bouncing down the ice towards me like a Barnes Wallis bomb, picking up speed, arms and legs everywhere. In that sort of situation a climber would normally try to get their ice axe into the slope to bring them to a halt or at least slow them down but I realised that John, a Royal Marine friend, had either lost his axe or was tumbling with so much force that he did not have a chance to use it. Either way, he was careering towards the edge of a serac, an ice cliff with a sheer drop of about 500m. He was close enough for me to see everything happen, almost in slow motion, but just too far away for me to do anything about it. I watched in horror as he bounced, slid then rolled past me about 15m away. I thought we'd lost him.

I don't know whether he hit loose snow or some other obstruction but suddenly John's roll towards the edge of the cliff slowed. He came to a halt just a couple of metres from the edge. He must have fallen, rolled, bounced and slid some 400m before he stopped and I fully expected he would be dead or badly injured. But as I tentatively traversed over the snow slope towards him he started moving, waved an arm and proclaimed himself okay!

The others came down and we checked him over; we could hardly believe he had escaped with just cuts and bruises. John is known for his toughness, resilience and good Royal Marine 'bootneck' characteristics but that was an extreme test of indestructibility. He dusted himself down with a quip about 'saving time and choosing a quick way down'. I have seen some close escapes in my time but that was about the nearest I had seen anyone come to certain death and survive. A few more metres and he would have gone over the edge.

The rest of the descent was uneventful. Unfortunately, however, the weather then closed in and I had to retreat to Base Camp after all, before I could bag Gasherbrum II. The others prepared to leave. I do not think they envied me hanging on in typically bad Karakoram weather. They kindly left me plenty of books to read, as well as lots of 24-hour ration packs. As a finale, the Joint Services Expedition held a little celebratory party before setting off back to the UK. After our joint ascent of Gasherbrum I, it would have been rude of me not to join them for a drink or two in the wilds of Pakistan, a country without a single pub or bar.

Camping at the side of the Shaksgam on a trek-in with camels on the north side of K2, China, 1994. From here we had to porter all our own equipment up the K2 Glacier. It took us two weeks to establish Base Camp.

THE TREK-IN

The trek to a base camp can be a mini expedition in itself. Many people visit the Himalaya or Karakoram purely for the trekking experience and some of the best routes – the Everest trek in Nepal, or the K2 trek in Pakistan, for example – go to the base camp of a major peak.

Most trek-ins to a base camp take between eight and ten days. Some, to more remote base camps such as those for K2 and the Gasherbrums in Pakistan, can take between 12 and 14. A few, such as the route to Nanga Parbat's low Base Camp above the Karakoram Highway, only take three or four days.

Hiring local porters to carry equipment and food beyond the road head helps local economies in areas without roads, where porters are the usual means by which goods are transported between villages. Mules or yaks are also sometimes available. Helicopters could be used to ferry supplies but that would be expensive and would contribute nothing to the local economy. Flying straight up to 5400m or higher is dangerous as you could rapidly become very ill or even die from acute mountain sickness (AMS). The trek-in is not only physically beneficial, allowing you to acclimatise slowly and properly, but it also helps psychologically as you can focus on the task ahead after all the hassle of organising an expedition.

Trekking in to Base Camp in Nepal can be a pleasure. It is a beautiful country and trekking routes generally start through villages connected by winding hill trails. Locals are usually very friendly and hospitable. In the lower foothills, where you might walk through terraced fields of rice and maize, it can be hot and you'll often experience afternoon rains, sometimes accompanied by dramatic thunderstorms. Higher up, the agriculture switches to barley and potatoes. Deeper into the mountains you leave the villages behind, perhaps finding remote dwellings selling tea or even cola and beer. Slowly the terrain gets rougher, more remote and colder as you approach Base Camp.

Treks can sometimes be testing or dangerous, especially if snow falls on a high pass or you have to traverse areas exposed to rock fall or avalanche. Also the monsoon can make things more challenging and just unpleasant – not only is it hot and wet but leeches are prolific.

I enjoy base camp treks. All the baggage of a western lifestyle can be cast aside. Why worry about whether you have paid the electricity bill or cancelled the milk? I read a lot of books and adopt a steady pace, enjoying the sights, smells and natural sounds, well away from any road noise. There is no rush. A bimble is better than a bash when it comes to acclimatisation.

Treks allow me to relax and get fitter before the big climbing effort. I can begin to concentrate properly on the task in hand – climbing and surviving an 8000m peak.

The South West Ridge from the Gasherbrum Glacier at 6200m. Looking up the 1800m South Face, the route can be followed up the ridge left of centre, across the snow under the rock triangle and back left to the summit.

8 GASHERBRUM II
8035M, 1996

'Bed tea. Chai. Good morning!'

My Base Camp cook was unzipping my tent door to thrust in a steel mug of steaming warm tea and a one-litre refill flask. The snow outside was six inches deep so I snuggled back into my down sleeping bag as I listened to the BBC World Service on my short wave radio and continued reading *Crow Road*, my second Iain Banks novel, hot on the heels of finishing *Complicity*. Both books are set in Scotland and it was nice to imagine myself there as I lay reading snugly in my tent.

The early morning light filtering through the falling snow was whitish-grey and opaque. Sounds seemed muffled and, listening to the soft swish of snow sliding down the tent flysheet, I felt a sense of tranquillity and comfort. It was nearly 7am and I was having a lie-in for another quarter of an hour. In this weather, I was going nowhere.

After climbing Gasherbrum I, my plan had been to go straight to its slightly lower neighbour, Gasherbrum II, without returning to Base Camp. Unfortunately the weather deteriorated, with fresh snowfall most days, thick cloud and high winds on the mountain. It was frustrating. All I could do for about three weeks was rest, eat, drink, read, listen to the World Service and generally try not to lose too much fitness.

My friends in the Joint Services GI team had packed up and left and I was now the only Brit around. I wandered over to visit other camps a couple of times and had a trek down to Concordia but it was a waiting game. I had to be ready at short notice for an improvement in the weather.

Luckily for me Richard Celsi, my friend from K2 in 1995, was leading an American expedition on GII and had set up camp close to mine. Most of his team had psyched out and gone home, unable to take the stress of hanging around,

digging tents out of the fresh snow most days and simply waiting and hoping for a settled spell of weather. Most days there were dumps of 30cm or more.

Waiting out bad weather in a base camp about the size of a couple of football pitches is not easy. After all, there's no chance of nipping to a takeaway, the cinema or even going climbing at the weekend. The desire to get up that mountain needs to be strong, as it always is for me, or you'll probably crack and give up. Patience helps, along with an ability to chill out. Luckily, I do enjoy reading good books and listening to the World Service.

Richard had a spacious mess tent – a 2m dome large enough to stand up in – and plenty of food. He invited me to join him, which made hanging out on the desolate

rock-strewn strip of ice a bit more fun. Richard had plenty of anecdotes as well as some very poignant tales from the Vietnam War, during which he had been decorated for bravery. Like me, he was into real coffee and rock music and he had a sound system with big speakers. There might have been a blizzard raging outside but inside we would be blasting out Led Zeppelin and drinking freshly ground coffee. A rock-coffee high at altitude! I wondered whether the Indian military could hear us on the other side of the Line of Control and what they made of the Pakistan Army's taste in music! The combination of loud music and Rich's lurid combat recollections put me in mind of scenes from *Apocalypse Now*.

A couple of times Rich and I made sorties through the bad weather, up the glacier towards Gasherbrum II. We would leave Base Camp with head torches at about two in the morning, full of caffeine and Led Zep. It was good to keep fit and usually involved several hours climbing and trekking through the heavily crevassed glacier. I left a small tent at about 6200m, below Gasherbrum II.

My original plan had been to solo the mountain but now I had the chance to rope up with Rich. We got on so well together that it seemed only natural. When our chance came to make an attempt on the summit, I set off with lines from Led Zep songs buzzing in my head – 'Communication breakdown', 'Good times, bad times, you know I had my share...', 'In the days of my youth I was told what it means to be a man...' – until the effort of pushing up the glacier towards the mountain drove them out of my brain.

Unfortunately, it seemed that the waiting in Base Camp had weakened Richard. He did not feel powerful enough for a summit attempt and soon turned back. In the circumstances it was the correct decision. There is no point struggling to 8000m only to find that you have no power left to get back down. I admire climbers who know their limits and who are able to retreat and survive.

Now I was alone again, soloing Gasherbrum II. It felt good and the weather was set fair.

The mountain is often dubbed a soft-touch 8000er. It is the lowest of the 14 which makes the altitude slightly

Left

High on the slopes. Masherbrum
(K1) 7821m on the right in the
distance and Nanga Parbat 8125m
in the far distance on the right.

less of a problem. But there is no such thing as a soft-touch 8000er. GII is still in the death zone. It is a remote mountain at the end of a long, dangerous approach from Base Camp with many crevasses. Huge avalanche-prone snow and ice slopes must be ascended and the Karakoram weather – worse than that in the Himalaya – must also be factored in. Some stretches demand a lot of trail breaking up snow slopes and I could have done with a climbing partner to help with this exhausting task. Sometimes there can be a hard, breakable crust with soft unconsolidated snow underneath, making for frustrating and debilitating terrain. Sinking calf deep or sometimes knee deep into the snow is strength sapping and it requires a determined perseverance to break trail in such conditions.

The lower part of the route climbed a snowy rib to about 7500m, where I scraped and dug out a small platform in the snow slope to pitch a tiny, single skin Gore-Tex one-man bivouac tent. The weather was crystal clear, with little or no wind, and I had fabulous views across the Karakoram to Masherbrum (K1) and beyond. In the far distance, I was sure that I could see Nanga Parbat at the western end of the Himalaya. I settled into melting snow for water using my little gas stove, resting and preparing for the final ascent. The route above did not look particularly steep or difficult and I was confident that the climbing would be well within my capabilities. Climbing alone, however, is a bigger psychological challenge and in the back of my mind I was perturbed by the avalanche risk.

Opposite

Climbers on the initial section of
the South West Ridge and South
Face, first climbed in 1956 by an
Austrian expedition. The summit,
at 8035m, is at the apex of the
triangular rock face, 1700m above.

In bitterly cold thin light, just after dawn, I flattened the tiny tent and covered it with snow blocks to prevent it blowing away. The final 500m to the summit continued up the ridge before the route broke off right across a steep snowfield, traversing under the summit pyramid above a thousand-metre drop to the glacier. I became aware of the avalanche danger as I punched holes in the slope, perforating the surface layers like toilet paper ready to rip. Fortunately the slope held and I reached another snow rib, crossed an open snowfield then a final rib leading to the top.

On the way up I passed a body wrapped in the remains of a tent. Plastic mountain boots with crampons attached and tattered clothing were protruding from the fabric. Climbing alone, I had plenty of time to dwell on that sad sight and it reinforced my determination not to underestimate the ascent. It might not have been technically demanding – there were no really steep, difficult sections – but it could still be lethal. Every mountain must be given its due respect.

The weather had, amazingly, stayed completely fine. It was flat calm and very clear. Looking past Gasherbrum III, Gasherbrum IV and Broad Peak, I could make out K2, and, looking the other way, Gasherbrum I. The upper section of Gasherbrum II is a beautiful classic pyramid of rock and snow. As summits go, it is one of the finest I have been on. It felt like a giant eagle's nest. I was on a tiny, flat snow platform about 2m by 1m with drops of nearly 2000m peeling off on all four sides and spectacular views to K2. The exposure was dizzying. I was determined not to become a sacrifice to the Karakoram peak by lingering too long but I did try to relish the panorama. I had a rest, then arranged a self-timer photo, manoeuvring tentatively around the summit eyrie. It was no place to slip.

Being alone in the flat calm conditions was weird; it somehow felt as alien and windless as the Moon. I was not used to such benign conditions at 8000m. The weather looked as if it was going to hold – no problem there – but I was slightly anxious about the continuing risk of avalanche on the steep slopes below as I prepared to descend.

I don't usually carry a walkie-talkie to a summit. With no chance of helicopters or rescue teams they are redundant extra weight, unless you like chatting. You can't eat them! For some reason, however, on this occasion I had taken Rich's walkie-talkie with me. Perhaps I derived some comfort from the fact that I could talk to another person despite climbing solo. I made a call to Base Camp

'Alan to BC. Over.'

Pakistan Army Captain Abrar, my liaison officer, answered. 'Go ahead Mr Alan, over.'

I replied, 'Abrar, it's me, Alan. I'm on top Gasherbrum II. Over.'

Abrar: 'Well done Mr Alan, I am so happy, so happy. But now, tell me, can – you – see – any – Indian – Army – positions – over – border? Over.'

Captain Abrar was a great liaison officer, one of the friendliest I had ever met, but he could not forget that he was a Pakistan Army Officer. He seriously expected me to spy on Indian Army positions! As I have Indian Army friends that would have put me in a tricky spot. I chose to ignore the request. I could not see anything anyway. I was only interested in the mountains and now needed to concentrate on getting down safely.

Descending, as expected, required more attention than the ascent. Lowering myself tentatively over the edge of the summit shelf on my belly, I faced in to the steep snow slope, climbing down the same way I had climbed up. As I got a bit lower, I was able to turn out and descend some sections facing out although a single stumble on a snow-clogged crampon would have meant a 1500m slide to oblivion. I crossed back over the snow basin below the summit pyramid and traversed across to the slightly safer ribs leading to my bivvy tent.

Since I had left my tent, the snow blocks pinning it down had melted and refrozen, gluing the blocks of ice to the tent. Nothing is ever easy on an 8000m peak I thought, as I hacked away at it like a convict in a chain gang. It was exhausting but I needed to get to my stove to melt some snow for a brew of tea, or at least some water. Two hours of precious pre-darkness descent time was used digging out the tent and my equipment but once I had rehydrated slightly I was able to continue all the way to Base Camp for some well-earned *dudh chai*, *dhal bhat* and a blast of Led Zeppelin.

The summit eyrie, 29 July 1996. Broad Peak and K2 behind.

Main photo
Looking back up at my steps that I have plugged in the snow as I descend alone from the summit of Gasherbrum II. These last few metres of very steep snow to the summit were extremely exposed with a 1700m-drop below my feet to the glacier.

Self-timer photo on top of Gasherbrum II, 29 July 1996. K2 is behind on the right. I had solo climbed Gasherbrum II and was alone on the summit. It was an amazing viewpoint, looking around at the giant peaks of the Karakoram in the clear, flat calm afternoon weather. I spent half an hour sitting on top of this exposed, tiny platform that was only slightly bigger than a double bed. I doubt that I contemplated the fact that I had now climbed all four of the Karakoram 8000m giants, and eight 8000ers in total. Statistics would be far from my mind and more likely I was summoning up the mental and physical strength for my solo descent.

Enjoying the pleasures of Base Camp with a steel mug of milk tea, *dudh chiya* in Nepali. A lot of tea is drunk to keep fluid levels up and prevent dehydration. As is usual in Base Camp, I am wearing a down-filled duvet jacket and layers of fleece to keep warm. I often wear my headtorch, which is very useful when nipping outside the tent into the dark Himalayan night.

I do enjoy freshly ground coffee. Once I start trekking on an expedition, however, I turn to tea and have even started to appreciate it at home. Until recently I rarely touched the stuff in Britain, but I drink gallons on an expedition. Himalayan locals thrive on tea and drink it in many different ways, often adding spices, salt or even rancid yak butter. In Nepal it is known as *dudh chiya*, in Pakistan as *dudh chai* or *cha*.

Simply breathing in the rarefied air at altitude causes dehydration so keeping your fluid intake up is crucial. Dehydration can be a killer. At altitude it can cause your blood to become more viscous, which can lead to thrombosis and even death. A cup of tea could be a lifesaver.

It is interesting how tea varies, how it is brewed and how it is served in different areas. Himalayan locals mostly drink it hot, milky and very sweet. Sherpas often like it salty, while Tibetans lace it with rancid yak butter. It is difficult to describe how disgusting yak butter tea can taste if you're not used to it. Imagine someone's sweaty

COFFEE OR TEA?

socks brewed in your teapot. However unsavoury it might seem to us, many Tibetans and Sherpas seem to relish it.

In the Himalayan foothills tea tends to come vigorously boiled, with milk, sugar and perhaps herbs and spices such as cardamom or ginger. Some tea comes in hard blocks the size of a house brick, from which chunks are broken off to boil up. Even in the humid lowlands, a drink of hot tea can refresh and revive.

Up on the mountain I take teabags, which sometimes have to be used more than once if I am storm-bound and low

on supplies. Often I will brew the bags in a pan of bubbling hot water for a few minutes to achieve a better flavour, as the boiling water is not as hot as it would be lower down. The boiling point of water decreases the higher you go.

After a climb, on return to Base Camp, I associate the first mug of hot milky tea with a feeling of relief. I know that I am safe and can relax. I have often been asked what it feels like to have climbed an 8000er. My reply is that I only appreciate a true sense of achievement when I am safely back in Base Camp with a mug of warm tea.

The South Face is a 3000m big wall, one of the biggest and steepest in the world. I attempted it in 1987. Jet stream winds are ripping over the summit ridge making a roaring noise like a squadron of jets, October 1987.

9 LHOTSE

8516M, 1997

By the time I returned from the Gasherbrums, I was formulating a plan to climb all 14 of the 8000m peaks. The hardest and the highest, K2 and Everest, had been ticked off. I knew that continuing would be dangerous but I felt that I was capable of it. I had the necessary determination, skill, resilience and stamina and, having climbed eight, was now just over halfway.

At that time, only three or four climbers had succeeded on all 14 and only a handful of climbers had managed eight. It seemed a worthy challenge, although the outcome was uncertain and death a possibility. There is no doubt it was a selfish quest – after all, my daughter did not want her Dad to die or even be away on long expeditions – but sometimes we have to respond to a calling. I wanted to experience the ultimate test of physical and mental stamina and determination, with its inevitable life-and-death judgements.

When I had been climbing my first few 8000ers I had not even considered trying to do them all. It was enough of a challenge to climb and survive one big mountain at a time. I had spent three years on K2 attempts and climbed several new lines on 8000ers as well as ascending many other peaks of 7000m and 6000m, as well as Alpine guiding and climbing in South America. Now, with eight 8000m peaks climbed, I set myself the challenge of climbing all 14 and called it Challenge 8000. My original plan was to attempt the remaining six – Lhotse, Makalu, Kangchenjunga, Nanga Parbat, Annapurna and Dhaulagiri – in one year. Clearly that required financial and logistical back up, neither of which was easy to find with less than six months to go.

First of the final six was Lhotse, the fourth highest mountain, which lies very close to Everest. Translated, its name means South Peak. It is separated from Everest only by the South Col and shares the same walk in and Base Camp.

I had already attempted Lhotse in 1987. After climbing Shisha Pangma, my first 8000er, I went straight to Lhotse's South Face with the Pole Artur Hajzer and Mexican Carlos Carsolio to join Krzysztof Wielicki's Polish expedition to the unclimbed Himalayan big wall. I was fit, acclimatised and not fazed by the daunting scale of the South Face. It was where I wanted to be. Rising directly from Base Camp, Lhotse South Face is a 3000m wall of steep, vertical and overhanging rock, ice and snow. There is no Khumbu Icefall to negotiate as there is on the North West Face route through the Western Cwm. At that time, I had only climbed one 8000er yet I found myself attempting one of the 'last great problems'.

Raring to go, I teamed up with the redoubtable Krzysztof and spent several days on the wall, pushing out the route. Squashed into a small bivvy tent balanced on a tiny ledge, I learnt a lot from Krzysztof. Several of his toes had been amputated due to frostbite and he instilled in me a discipline to look after mine. Before we left the tent for a sub-zero, pre-dawn start, we would not only warm our feet but also our boots over the stove and a candle. It was difficult, slow and time-consuming in the cramped conditions, especially as altitude makes you feel lethargic.

Krzysztof is one of the greatest Himalayan climbers and it was a privilege to climb with him. He went on to become the fifth person to climb all the 8000m peaks.

We made good progress on Lhotse South Face and pushed the route up to over 8000m. It was like being on the North Face of the Eiger, with steep rock walls and ice fields raked by stone fall, only much higher in the Himalayan death zone.

We had nearly climbed the face and were poised for a summit bid when one of the worst post-monsoon storms of the decade engulfed the area. I had to abandon a lot of equipment and we were lucky to get down alive. We holed up in Base Camp for several days as avalanches poured down, smashing several tents and eventually forcing us to retreat to a stone shelter lower down. Close by, at Island Peak base, an avalanche hit the camp and killed several climbers. When the blizzards and snowfall stopped, a

roaring jet stream wind blasted the face. The incessant noise sounded like a squadron of jets and the wind strength made it impossible to move back on to the face. Most of our equipment had been smashed and ripped by the avalanches and storm force winds.

We were lucky to survive such a vicious storm and snowfall. A valiant effort was thwarted by the approach of winter cold and jet stream wind. I came to the view that it was probably better to climb an 8000er in the pre-monsoon season, when the jet stream was moving away and conditions improve slightly as the monsoon approaches.

Now, a decade on, I was planning to climb Lhotse's North West Face route, the steep gully of snow and ice I remembered seeing and photographing from the top of Everest.

Mal Duff, an old climbing friend, was heading there with an expedition to Everest and Lhotse. He was one of the pioneers of so-called commercial expeditions and had a team of fee-paying climbers attempting Everest and

Above

Artur Hajzer at 7300m on the South Face, at one of the precarious, tiny campsites. On this steep, dangerous big wall, you need a helmet to protect against falling rocks. At times it felt like being on a super-sized North Face of the Eiger.

Opposite

Makalu 8463m. The fifth highest mountain in the world seen from high on the South Face of Lhotse, the fourth highest.

the Lhotse route goes straight up, heading for the gully or couloir that tops out just below the summit.

Mal had extensive Himalayan experience and I met up with him in Kathmandu. It was good to catch up and I looked forward to spending some time at Base Camp and Advanced Base Camp with him. We even spoke about doing one of my remaining 8000ers together later in the year. I had a cameraman and director with me to film my trek to Base Camp, so I let Mal go ahead with his team and clients to set up the camp.

Once the film crew had shot some general Kathmandu footage, we set off as a three-man trekking team to Base Camp. I have been to the Khumbu a few times but the flight to Lukla never fails to impress or even scare at times. The runway is cut into the side of a mountain. It is somewhat like landing on an aircraft carrier except if you overshoot you crash into a mountainside.

From Lukla it is a two-day hike to Namche Bazaar, a Sherpa town built in a natural amphitheatre, with temples and prayer stupas (Buddhist shrines), like something from a Lost World movie. The Khumbu is the Sherpa region of Nepal and Namche is its capital. After a couple of nights' acclimatisation and rest here it is another five days or more to Base Camp. Unfortunately the cameraman was neither coping with the exercise nor acclimatising. He looked quite ill and had to go down. The director took over the filming as far as Base Camp but he only spent one night there before trekking out to leave me to get on with the climb and film myself as usual.

It was my first time at Everest's south side Base Camp, a much less desolate place than the Tibet Base Camp above Rongbuk. The north side is flat, rocky and dusty, whereas here we had to hack out flat tent spots in the undulating glacier ice, on which about two hundred people from various expeditions were clustered together. Were it not for the satellite dishes, the whole area might have resembled some medieval camp. The toilets, which help to keep the area clean, were basic middens, filling big blue barrels which porters would carry away down the valley to fertilise the fields. Not the best job in the world.

a few attempting Lhotse. Mal let me buy a place on his Lhotse ticket. I intended to solo the peak, but this saved me the expense of buying a full permit just for me. He also generously offered to share his Base Camp, Advanced Base Camp, Camp 1, Camp 2 and food with me, which helped with my logistics and costs.

The first part of the Lhotse climb is the same as that for Everest – through the infamous Khumbu Icefall, into the Western Cwm and up the Lhotse Face to a point almost at the South Col. Instead of traversing left to the South Col,

I planned to start up the same line taken by Edmund Hillary and Tenzing Norgay on the first Everest ascent in 1953. As on the north, the south side of Everest was steeped in history. I was looking forward with trepidation to climbing through the Khumbu Icefall. It has a fearsome reputation. It is a chaotic melée of tottering blocks of ice, some the size of six-storey buildings, cascading down the mountain. Throw a few deep crevasses, avalanches and rockfalls into that glacial cauldron of horror and it's clear that it is one of the ascent's most lethal sections.

Mal had been through the icefall before. Although the route had been fixed with ropes and ladders and it would have been no problem for me to go solo, Mal offered to climb up with me as far as Advanced Base Camp. Later that night, however, he began to feel unwell and said he could not come with me. I had been looking forward to Mal's company on that particularly dangerous section of the climb and we could have filmed each other. Never mind, I thought, it would do me good to climb and cope with the stress alone.

I left Base Camp just after dawn, to get through the icefall before the sun started to melt parts of it. I reached Camp 1 at about 9am. Calling down on the radio, I was shocked and felt sick at heart to be told that Mal had died in his tent. We had enjoyed a chat just the previous evening and he had tied a sacred *Puja* cord around my neck. He wore several himself from previous expeditions but reckoned the Dalai Lama had blessed the one he tied round my neck. It had been the last thing he had done before going to his bed. I was the last person to see Mal alive.

Deeply saddened, I returned to Base Camp where a memorial service for Mal was held before his body began its journey back to Kathmandu.

Everest 8848m, the final 900m climb from the South Col at 7920m, seen from high on the West Face of Lhotse. This is the south east ridge route first climbed in 1953 by Hillary and Tenzing. The South Summit and the Hillary Step can be seen high on the ridge, as well as yellow tents in a snow-free patch on the South Col. Although it's the 'easy' route, it looks worthy of respect.

I spent several days at Base Camp, coming to terms with his death. I have lost countless friends and acquaintances on the mountains and have come to regard it as an occupational hazard but Mal's death hit me hard. I had climbed with him since I was a teenager, on my first visits to Scotland. He was a great climber and a fantastic bloke. In the end I decided to stay on the mountain. Mal would not have wanted me to abandon my Lhotse climb.

After a few days' rest I retraced my steps through the icefall and into the Western Cwm – so named by British climbers in the 1950s who had done their pre-expedition training in Wales – at 6500m. Again, I made sure to set off pre-dawn, before the heat of the day destabilised the icefall.

With the South West Face of Everest to my left and Lhotse dead ahead, it struck me that I had already done most of the route for Everest and it would have been comparatively easy to get to the top again. If I ever climb Everest again, I think I will do it from Nepal, despite the Khumbu Icefall.

I was still thinking of Mal as I tried to rest at Advanced Base Camp, which was not easy. It felt as if the afternoon sun was sucking the air from this high-altitude valley. A very unpleasant condition known as 'glacier lassitude' can set in leaving the human body incapable of functioning. The altitude, the lack of oxygen and the excessive heat and cold contribute to a general bodily malaise as you become more and more debilitated. In effect, you are slowly dying.

Three Russian climbers follow me to the summit of Lhotse. Looking down loose shaley rock to the col at the top of the couloir.

The weather looked set to remain stable for a few days and I reckoned one more bivouac should see me to the top. The following day I climbed the Lhotse Face mingling with the many people going up Everest. The Everest and Lhotse routes coincided as far as Camp 3, ascending a steep icy snow slope to ledges scraped out for tents at 7500m. I rested there and set off at midnight for the final 1000m climb.

Initially I followed the Everest route a short way, then broke off right and directly up, heading for the snow gully on Lhotse's North West Face. The views across to the South Col and the South East Ridge of Everest were fantastic. I could see all the way up over the south summit and the Hillary Step to the top. Some refer to this so-called 'normal' route on Everest as a 'yak route'. All I can say is that it did not look like a walk to me.

Three Russians also attempting Lhotse caught me up. They had some rope, so I went ahead and fixed some to help with the descent. Fixing the rope cost extra time and slowed the ascent but I knew we would need it later to abseil back down. The gully was fairly steep – about Scottish Grade 2 – and I used nuts, ice-screws, pitons and slings to secure the rope. By the time I reached the summit it was late morning, nearly midday, and clouds were beginning to boil up from the Western Cwm. The Russians joined me on the summit and two of them lit a cigarette. I was gobsmacked. At 8500m there is hardly enough oxygen in the air to survive let alone to start smoking!

I had carried up my video camera so I filmed the Russians, shot some video clips and a couple of pieces to camera before I set off down. As there were now ropes in place to assist a fast descent, I felt I could stay on the summit a bit longer than usual, perhaps 15 to 20 minutes. I knew I was unlikely to come up here again – it was hardly the same as popping up Helvellyn in the Lake District – and I wanted to enjoy gazing at the view down the Western Cwm and over to Cho Oyu for a little longer.

Once I started down, I quickly caught up with and overtook the Russians. I kept going, down to the relative safety of Advanced Base Camp. Rather than descend the icefall that evening, I waited until the following morning when it was frozen and easier to walk on the snow.

No one was waiting for me in Base Camp. A couple of the Everest climbers congratulated me, as I did them on their Everest ascents. The Russians invited me to a party as two of them were mates from Nanga Parbat in 1992. But deep down I felt sad. I missed Mal.

Rather than walk out, I had arranged a helicopter to pick me up (despite the discouraging sight of a crashed helicopter near Base Camp). I intended to fly directly to my next 8000m peak, Makalu, where two friends had already set up Base Camp and were waiting for me. It was late May. I knew it would be touch-and-go to get to the summit. The high avalanche risk and approaching monsoon meant that I decided to retreat.

It only took half an hour to fly to Lukla – a welcome alternative to two or three days' yomping back. Skimming down the Khumbu in a heli, revelling in the mountain scenery was a great finale to climbing my ninth 8000er. Only five left.

Photo taken on my descent from the summit of Lhotse, looking up the steep couloir cutting through the West Face. This gully leads to a col, from where a short rocky climb leads to the summit. I remember noticing this distinct line from the top of Everest in 1996 and thinking that it looked like the obvious route up.

Dawa follows me up steep granite, Alpine-style climbing at 7500m approaching the Makalu La. My plastic high-altitude boot is covered with a gaiter and I have crampons on as the climbing is mixed rock and ice.

PHOTOGRAPHY & FILMING

I started using a camera and taking photos at an early age, with a 127 roll film camera, progressing to 35mm and developing my own black and white prints. Moving to colour transparency film exposure was more critical than with black and white print film, but I soon got a feel for interpreting a light meter reading and adjusting the shutter speed and F-stop. Film and processing was expensive and you never knew what you had got until it came back from the lab. Mostly I used non-process paid film, which meant that I could use a local lab and not risk my valuable images in the postal system.

Most of the cameras that I used were mechanical, usually range finder type, rather than SLR. For still photography I could take out 100 rolls of 36-exposure transparency film, which is a day sac full in volume and a lot of extra weight. En route this bulky cargo of film would be X-rayed many times and on the trek to Base Camp it could be cooked in the heat of the day and frozen at night. Not a recommended treatment for producing the best quality images.

All this quantity of film is now replaced by a couple of small memory cards that can be safely X-rayed. Happy days.

All digital cameras are electronic and rely on batteries, but I keep them warm next to my body and bring them out briefly for taking photos. On Kangchenjunga in the gloomy light just before dark my new digital camera proved its worth capturing a great arm's length summit photo, using fill-in flash and auto focus.

Film-making used to be more arduous. 16mm cameras had only two minutes of film and no sound, unless a separate audio recorder was used. I made 13 half hour documentaries on my expeditions initially using 16mm and Hi-8 video before mini DVC.

Taking photos and filming always adds to the risk, slowing down the climb, and handling a camera in sub zero temperatures increases the likelihood of frostbite. I filmed myself, either at arm's length or balancing the camera on a rock ledge, climbing past it and returning to retrieve it, which meant I had climbed that section three times.

Descending Makalu, I had a near miss filming my climbing partner, Dawa. Concentrating on my camera work I had let my guard down. Becoming slightly complacent, I forgot about the precarious position I was in. Balancing on my crampon points above a 1000m-drop, I slipped, but luckily a rope I had clipped into held, saving my life. It was a close shave.

10 NANGA PARBAT
8125M, 1998

The Sanskrit name for Nanga Parbat 8125m means Naked Mountain, possibly because it stands alone at the western end of the Himalaya in Pakistan. It was the first 8000er to be attempted in 1895, by British mountaineer Alfred Mummery who disappeared on the peak. Since then it has developed a notorious reputation because of the high number of fatalities on early attempts which led it to become known as the Killer Mountain. Unlike other 8000ers, Base Camp is on grass at 4200m, a relatively low altitude and more pleasant to live at, however that means there is a greater height to climb to the summit. The massive 4000m Diamir Face rises directly from the grassy meadows. The Kinshofer Route starts up the broad couloir left of the toe of the central buttress.

I felt the shuddering vibration and heard the roar of a huge rock avalanche, drumming like the hooves of a hundred galloping horses, as it swept down the gully and engulfed me. Stones bounced and scraped off my helmet as blocks the size of cars and fridge-freezers exploded next to me, showering me in rock shrapnel.

It was like being in a slow-motion nightmare. I had nowhere to hide. I expected an enormous block to crush me or rip off my arm with a glancing blow and became resigned to my fate. In the end, the maelstrom lasted only about 15 or 20 seconds but it seemed much longer. Escaping unscathed, physically at least, I was then able to scramble to a ledge, collapse and relieve my panic-stricken bladder.

That was back in 1992, during my first attempt on Nanga Parbat, the Killer Mountain. I was with six others, including Doug Scott, two Russians and two Nepalis and we intended to climb a difficult route known as the Mazeno Ridge. But another rock avalanche badly injured one of the two Russians and so we had to rescue him, get him down to Base Camp and abort the expedition. It was a real baptism of fire on the notoriously dangerous mountain.

Nanga Parbat was the first 8000m peak ever to be attempted, by the Victorian mountaineer Alfred Mummery in 1895. He perished in the attempt, along with two Gurkhas. It has been no less benign since and has earned a reputation for difficulty and danger from avalanche, rock fall and severe storms. On two Austro-German expeditions, in 1934 and 1937, 26 people were killed and Nanga Parbat was dubbed the Killer Mountain. In 1939, another Austro-German expedition set out to attempt it. Its members were interned on the outbreak of World War II but Heinrich Harrer escaped to Tibet. His adventures were published as the classic book, later a film,

Looking down the moraine-strewn Diamir Glacier, towards Chilas in the Indus valley and the Karakoram Highway. This road runs through Pakistan to China, from Islamabad to Kashgar. Base Camp tents can be seen on the grass above the glacier on its true right bank.

Seven Years in Tibet. German and Austrian interest in the peak continued after World War II, in a similar way to British interest in Everest. Eventually the inspirational Austrian climber Hermann Buhl made the first ascent in 1953.

On my second attempt I had a bizarre, and subsequently infamous incident involving a chapatti. I sneezed on some burnt crust or flour that had blown up my nose and suffered a slipped disc. I was in agony for several days before I managed to crawl and stagger to a lower altitude, where a heli could evacuate me to Islamabad for initial treatment. Earlier I had strained my back lifting heavy loads while organising the expedition equipment. I was probably weakened by the fact that it was my seventh expedition to an 8000m peak within 12 months. Being at extreme altitude so many times in such a short period is debilitating and had stripped my body of some of its muscle. I was wasting away. The specialist at Shifa hospital in Islamabad told me that a sneeze or cough is a common way to prolapse a disc after an initial muscle strain but he couldn't resist a chuckle over the fact that a humble chapatti had caused the sneeze. Nor could the British media.

Back in Britain I faced a long fight back to fitness, involving serious physiotherapy and rock climbing to strengthen my back. I was determined to return to Pakistan and climb Nanga Parbat.

To complicate matters further, in late May I was involved in a car crash and broke several ribs. Even that did not deter me and in June I flew to Islamabad. My plan was to spend a couple of weeks cycling, walking and swimming in the Margalla Hills, slowly letting the painful ribs heal before I set off for Base Camp. I had to cycle up the hills out of Islamabad in the early morning before sunrise, as by 10am it could be over 35°C and very humid. Cycling on the hot black tarmac up the steep hairpin bends in the Margalla Hills made an excellent cardiovascular workout. It would have been a good hill session on the Tour de France and I wondered how cycle-fit I must have been getting.

I decided to solo Nanga Parbat but shared the cost of a Pakistan Ministry of Tourism permit with an Italian group. I was totally independent with a separate Base Camp and the Italian expedition, which included the legendary Kurt Diemberger, travelled ahead of me. Diemberger had made the first ascents of Broad Peak in 1957 and Dhaulagiri in 1960. I had met him a couple of times before and it was great to be on a mountain with him, although by now he was 66 years old and I wasn't sure how serious he was about a summit bid. Nevertheless we climbed together on the lower slopes as I acclimatised, and shared a bivouac on one occasion.

It was late June before I reached Base Camp, which was set on a pleasant grassy meadow at the relatively low altitude of 4100m. The local villagers and porters remembered me from the previous year and were pleased that I had returned fit and well to climb their mountain. As usual they were all kitted out with AK47s so I could not refuse their fresh chapattis.

The climb on the 4000m Diamir Face above Base Camp becomes vertical almost immediately, with lots of loose and dangerous sections of rock. While I was there, a member of a Japanese expedition was killed in a rock fall.

On my first sortie I left base at 1am with a 20kg rucksack for an Alpine-style ascent. Not yet fully acclimatised,

I took nine hours to climb the 1000m Kinshofer Gully and overhanging 200m Kinshofer Wall. The gully is a calf-burning, steep slope of snow and ice, strafed by stone fall. It is an extremely risky place to be, particularly after sunrise when the ice above begins to melt. Rocks smash onto the slope like incoming mortar fire. It is no place for the faint hearted and best ascended pre-dawn while the rock is mostly frozen. I had to climb the gully two or three times to acclimatise myself, the intensity of the danger sapping some of my psychological energy.

As well as overhanging, the final wall is loose, strenuous and intimidating. Tatty old ropes and caving ladders made of thin wire and alloy rungs dangle precariously. Most are unsafe to pull up on or use in any way and are just another hazard to contend with on the taxing climb. Once up that section, I was able to dig out a relatively safe bivouac site at 5800m, only a little higher than base camps on most 8000m mountains. Above, interesting mixed rock, ice and snow climbing leads to vast snow and ice fields below the final summit slopes, all exposed to plenty of avalanche risk.

Three weeks after arriving in Base Camp, I felt ready for the summit push. I had already been to 6300m and stashed a tiny supply of food, gas and a bivouac shelter. The weather seemed to have settled into a pattern of fine early mornings followed by afternoon snow showers. The avalanche potential and climbing conditions were as good as they would get and I felt fit and ready to make a summit attempt. My sixth sense signals felt right.

I made another frightening push up the dangerous Kinshofer Gully, with a few other climbers who were also making a summit bid. Later on 20 July, I struggled for more than 12 hours through waist-deep snow enduring a blizzard and near-whiteout storm. It took until 5pm to arrive at 7100m and a spot flat enough for a bivouac. I was not sure that I had enough power left to make a summit attempt.

An airborne powder snow avalanche roars down the Diamir Face opposite tents, which are tucked under a rock buttress for protection on the Kinshofer Route.

I tried to rest and rehydrate, melting snow for water, huddled inside my tiny bivouac with spindrift seeping inside. Later that night, the wind eased. I had to seize my chance for the summit. It was 3am before I could set off in the extreme -30°C chill of pre-dawn. Starting off with six others, I immediately found the going tough, with deep fresh snow slowing progress. With my feet constantly buried inside the cold white mass, frostbite was a real concern. That final 1000m, west-facing summit slope does not get any sun until the afternoon, making Nanga Parbat a particularly cold climb.

I was breaking trail a lot of the time. It was extremely hard work and as I struggled in the deep snow I knew it would be late afternoon, perhaps close to sunset before I reached the top. Going down was probably the sensible option, yet I was so close... I realised that if I retreated I might not get another chance that year. In the early afternoon we were engulfed by a blizzard. Spindrift poured down the slopes,

Above

Climber in the dangerous rock-strafed Kinshofer Couloir at 4800m on the initial section of the Diamir Face. Several people have been injured and killed on this part of the climb; while I was there a Japanese climber was hit by stone-fall near this spot and killed.

Right

Vertical and overhanging rock above the col 4900m at the top of the Kinshofer Couloir. Once this extremely steep section is overcome to Camp 1 at 5100m, the rest of the Diamir Face is mostly snow and ice climbing.

filling in our tracks as the storm battered all seven of us for three or four hours. I steeled myself to push on through the blizzard, sure that it was only an afternoon storm as the weather seemed set in that sort of pattern. Had it been a monster of a storm, lasting for several days, we would surely have perished whether we went up or down.

The others followed me and we finally broke through the cloud only half an hour from the summit although it was now 6pm and not far off dark. Through gaps in the cloud I caught glimpses of Base Camp and the Diamir Valley, already in deep shade. At 6.30pm we were in the alpenglow on the summit. I snatched a summit photo with my picture of Fiona, filmed a short video sequence and headed down into the darkness.

I was prepared for a descent in the dark with a head torch and two spare batteries but I was not relishing the prospect. Some of the others were not as prepared and I knew an epic was on the cards.

I became aware that the slope back to my bivouac at 7100m was massively loaded with afternoon snowfall. Leading the descent I anxiously pushed ahead to find the route down the avalanche-prone slope. There were no tracks to follow and snow was sliding off around me like caster sugar. I was scared but had no option other than to press on down in the dark, mustering my skill and experience to seek out the best line. Fate and good fortune prevailed and the straggling group of climbers followed my tracks safely down the summit snowfield.

Around midnight, I stopped very close to my bivouac and the couple of other tents clustered on the small flattish spot at 7100m. I could just make them out, but it was difficult to find the safe route in the dark, even with my head torch. I was only 100m from the shelter of my tent but I felt it was too dangerous to break trail solo, unroped, through deep crevasses now hidden under fresh snow. I decided to wait for a couple of the others, intending to tie into their rope and cross safely. Unfortunately the wait lasted more than two harrowingly cold, dark hours, before two of them arrived at 2am. When I tried to explain why I had stopped they did not seem to understand and when I suggested getting their

rope out they told me they were so exhausted that they had ditched it to save weight.

Resigned to my fate, I expected to have to wait until daylight before we would be able to see where the strongest and safest snow bridges offered a safe route to the haven of the tents. However, without a word, one of the other climbers wearily shuffled forward into the gloom. I was amazed at his foolhardy recklessness – or was it bravery? He told me later that he felt he had no other option, as the cold, dehydration and sheer exhaustion had just about finished him anyway. If he had broken through a snow bridge, he would have been killed.

But he did not disappear into a crevasse and so I followed, spotted the safe route and ten minutes later, after hanging around in -30°C for nearly three hours, I was at my tent struggling to get my crampons off before collapsing inside.

Descending at sunset from the summit into the gloom of the Diamir Face, with the valley 4000m below already in darkness.

The climb to the summit and back from that tiny tent at 7100m had taken 22 hours but, as worn out as I was, I still had a long way to go back down to the safety of Base Camp. Later that morning, in full daylight, I packed up and descended further to the top of the steep Kinshofer Wall at 5800m. After yet another bivouac, I made an early start to abseil down before the sun rose, relieved that it would be absolutely the last time I would risk the rock fall in the Kinshofer Gully.

With a great feeling of elation, relief and pleasure I finally approached the haven of Base Camp, the horror of Nanga Parbat forever behind me. Arriving in camp, Rehman, my Pakistani cook, had my usual mug of warm milky tea without sugar ready for me. After several refills of the reviving milky brew I got stuck into a plate of fried eggs, chips and warm fresh chapattis spread liberally with butter. Life felt good in the grassy meadow below the Killer Mountain. I had, I mused, now climbed ten of the 8000ers. Only four remained. Challenge 8000 was looking more achievable.

KURT DIEMBERGER

Austrian Kurt Diemberger is one of only two people to have made first ascents of two 8000m peaks. The other, Hermann Buhl, was killed on Chogolisa in Pakistan's Karakoram, in June 1957. Kurt was the last person to see Hermann before he fell through a cornice on the summit ridge.

Kurt and Willie Bauer were the only two survivors of the 1986 K2 tragedy in which five climbers perished during a storm that raged from 6 to 10 August. The seven were trapped at 7900m. Kurt suffered severe frostbite and had several fingers and toes amputated. In total, 13 died on K2 between June and August that year, including leading British mountaineer Alan Rouse and Kurt's British climbing partner, Julie Tullis. Extreme altitude is very unforgiving. Al was a friend and a brilliant climber and I found it hard to believe that he could not have struggled down like Kurt.

I first met Kurt in Kathmandu in the late 1980s, when I was climbing with Polish friends of his. It was like meeting a living Himalayan legend. I noticed his shortened fingers and resolved to keep mine. We have since met at various mountain festivals but also, more notably, on Nanga Parbat in 1998. At the time it seemed strange that, despite then being in his mid-60s, he was attempting a challenge such as Nanga Parbat, known as the Killer Mountain. Perhaps Kurt was there because his friend Hermann Buhl had made the first ascent back in 1953.

I spent some time chatting with him in Base Camp and at above 6000m on the mountain. He had many interesting and poignant stories to tell but I never pressed him on the K2 tragedy. We drank tea and chatted about 8000ers in general, climbers we both knew and famous mountaineers that Kurt knew, such as Reinhold Messner. Hearing a first hand account of the first ascent of Broad Peak was a thrill and a privilege for me, and his anecdotes about great 1950s mountaineers such as Fritz Wintersteller, Marcus Schmuck and Buhl were captivating. We also mused about the weather and conditions on Nanga Parbat looming above Base Camp and our chances of climbing it. I was impressed that he still wanted to summit that big, dangerous mountain. Clearly, mountains arc in his soul.

Legendary Austrian mountaineer Kurt Diemberger at Camp 1 5100m on Nanga Parbat in 1998. Kurt made a strong attempt on Nanga Parbat. It was amazing to think he had climbed with Herman Buhl, who made the first ascent of Nanga Parbat in 1953 and that he was with Buhl when he disappeared on Chogolisa in 1957.

11 MAKALU

8463M, 1999

The readout showed an altitude of 8000m and a temperature of -45°C. I took another sip of champagne and relaxed as the Qatar Airways Airbus cruised through the upper atmosphere. Just two weeks earlier I had also been at extreme altitude on the summit of Makalu at 8463m. The temperature had been a balmy -35°C back then but I had a difficult descent to deal with rather than a reclining seat in Business Class.

Makalu had not succumbed easily. It took several attempts. My first was in 1988 with Doug Scott and friends. I nearly made it to the top when, close to the summit, my climbing partner Rick Allen was avalanched and swept down 400m. He was very lucky to survive, albeit with head wounds and his nose badly damaged. It was a bloody scene when I reached him but luckily he is a tough character and I managed to improvise a rescue to help him down to Base Camp.

On another attempt in 1995, I slipped off the path en route to Base Camp. A tree stopped me plummeting 60m to my death but one of the branches ripped into my leg like a medieval spear. The branch narrowly missed my femoral artery – otherwise I would have bled to death – and fortunately missed other vital bits – otherwise I might have been singing soprano. I was in the Himalayan foothills, five days from the nearest road, and my infected leg urgently needed medical treatment. My Nepali friend and trekking agent, Bikrum Pandi, was contacted by satellite phone and, as I was below the 6500m flight ceiling, a heli was sent the next day to whisk me to a clinic in Kathmandu. A local villager in the same predicament would have had to be carried to the road head, and might well have died en route. Luckily, I was insured through the British Mountaineering Council so all my rescue and medical costs were underwritten.

Tents on the Makalu La at 7500m, on the 1988 Doug Scott-led expedition, with Lhotse, the South Col and Everest behind. Gauri Shankar and Menlungtse can be seen in the far distance. In spring 1988 I made the first ascent of the West Face of Menlungtse with Andy Fanshawe.

The American doctor in Kathmandu joked about cutting my leg off – I appreciated the black humour and irony – he then recommended that I left Kathmandu for treatment, as it was a serious and infected wound. To travel back to the UK in that state would be too much, so to save my leg I was transferred to Bangkok for surgery. I spent three weeks in hospital there before returning to the UK and regained enough fitness to climb K2 that same year.

In 1997, I made yet another attempt on Makalu after climbing Lhotse but was foiled that time by poor conditions. Some thought that Makalu was becoming my bogey mountain and that I might never get up it.

Makalu, the fifth highest peak in the world, was first climbed by the great French mountaineers Lionel Terray and Jean Couzy in 1955. It has always been known as one of the more difficult 8000ers. With a long approach trek, a high base camp, exposed and avalanche-prone slopes and sections of technical climbing, it is no easy nut to crack.

I headed for Makalu again in 1999, planning another solo attempt as I had on GI, GII, Lhotse and Nanga Parbat. Trekking in to Base Camp, I fell seriously ill with a virulent strain of giardia, a nasty intestinal infection, and was helicoptered back to Kathmandu. Recovering in the smog and heat of the city, I felt sick with disappointment. I knew that even if I got better in a week, getting back to Base Camp would take so long that I would run out of time to climb Makalu before the monsoon hit.

In the end a sponsor, Britannia Movers International, covered the cost of a heli to ferry me part way back to Base Camp. I was dropped off at 3500m, not far from Lower Base Camp at 5000m, but rather than rush up and give myself altitude sickness I spent three days moving up slowly and acclimatising.

Left

Near Makalu Base Camp crossing the milky glacial meltwater stream issuing from the glacier at 4800m in the Barun Valley. The 3400m South East Face of Makalu towers above.

My equipment and cook were waiting for me. It was now late April and I only had four weeks left to acclimatise properly, get fit and tackle the mountain before my permit expired on 31 May and the monsoon moved up from the Bay of Bengal to engulf the peak in snow.

I had originally hoped to summit by around 15 May but I was not too perturbed. From years of experience I knew that there was usually a good weather window at the end of the month, between the 23rd and the 29th.

Makalu was in good condition after a dry winter, with little snow build-up and an unusually low avalanche risk. I made a couple of acclimatisation forays higher and set up Advanced Base Camp at 5700m which is, in reality, the true Base Camp used by most expeditions. From there I intended to climb Alpine-style solo to the summit.

Although I had intended to climb alone, my Nepalese sirdar and friend Dawa Chirring, whom I had known since 1996, kept hinting that he also wanted to climb the peak. He had never summited an 8000er although he had been high on Everest. It would be safer crossing crevasses roped together and also psychologically easier with a climbing partner. We got on well together, so I agreed to share the climb. If he succeeded on Makalu, he would be able to find work as a climbing Sherpa on Everest, which is a very well-paid job in Nepal.

By 5 May we had pushed up, Alpine-style, to the Makalu La at 7400m, where we spent a fitful night acclimatising. The next day we descended to Base Camp to recover for a couple of days before returning to make a summit bid. However, as is often the case on big mountains, it was not to be that simple. The weather closed in and jet stream winds tore into the mountain, pinning us down. With the wind

Right

Nga Temba, our sirdar, third from the left at the foot of the rock, in blue salopettes, organises porters for the trek to Makalu Base Camp in 1988 with the Doug Scott expedition. These hardy Nepalese porters carry 25kg loads to Base Camp.

roaring like a hundred jumbo jets, I expected that the little tent left up on the mountain would be ripped to shreds and blown away. Inside was all my summit push equipment and if the tent had been destroyed my climb would be over. The storms and bad weather continued for two weeks. All I could do was hang out, read, listen to the radio and wait.

Makalu was really testing and trying me again. I worried that the slopes would be avalanche-prone when we went back up as fresh snow lay over the old hard ice slopes.

I started to clear my head and prepare my body for a taxing summit push. A lot of the effort on an 8000m peak is psychological. Determination and resilience are essential but knowing when to turn back is crucial for survival.

On 21 May, Dawa and I pushed back up through deep snow to the Makalu La. Our tiny tent had survived and we huddled inside, melting snow for water to rehydrate ourselves. My instincts told me that we now had a chance. I felt ready and Makalu seemed to have settled down. Next day we moved up another 400m of technically easy snow and ice slopes to bivouac at 7800m. We hacked a ledge out of the 45° ice slope and squashed uncomfortably together, trying to rest before the summit push. Sleep was not possible at -35°C and we concentrated on the tiresome, arduous but essential task of melting snow for water and tea.

At about 5.30am on 23 May, Dawa and I set off on our summit bid. Perhaps we should have left earlier in the dark but I was trying to get a feel for the conditions and weather before committing myself. Initially we climbed unroped, taking turns to break trail up the steep snow and ice slope. At around 8100m, we traversed left towards a rock rib, which led to the summit arête. There we passed the body of a Danish climber, frozen into the slope. He had fallen from near the summit three weeks previously. When he was alive I had met him at Everest Base Camp and several times in Kathmandu where we had drunk a beer together. He was a nice chap. It was a sad sight and I resolved to take extra care on the descent.

In the midst of life there is death, as they say, and that is amplified in high-altitude mountaineering. It is upsetting when someone dies but I have never understood why, to some climbers, it comes as such a shock. If you are going to

climb big mountains, you have to accept that some people are going to perish. The key to staying alive is improving your odds as much as you can by making the right decisions on those factors that are within your control. Attention to detail is critical.

We were both in good spirits, Dawa because he was so close to completing his first 8000er, me because things had gone well and I was within a few hundred metres of my 11th. Dawa was certainly strong and determined enough but still very inexperienced, so we roped up and I took the

Above the clouds on the airy knife-edge ridge to the summit. With a drop of 3000m to Base Camp, Dawa rests on the final exposed section, before following me to the summit.

lead as the climbing became rockier. Back in Britain such climbing would have been easy on warm, sunny rock. At well above 8000m, with the temperature at -25°C, even pulling up on big handholds was difficult and I had to gasp for oxygen in the thin air. I was strangely enjoying it. On a couple of the ledges I came across a few large steel oxygen bottles, engraved 'CAF Himalayan Expedition Makalu 1955', left behind by the French Club Alpin Français during the first ascent. It felt like finding archaeological remains and I would have loved one as a souvenir. But they weighed about 5kg and I left them where they were.

I could see Everest and Lhotse, 15–20km away, starting to disappear in a huge mushroom and anvil-shaped cloud. They were engulfed within a maelstrom of a storm and it looked like it was heading towards us. The wind started to gust, spindrift blasted my face and the oh-so-close summit of Makalu became shrouded in cloud. I felt sick with frustration as the weather closed in. Much tricky climbing remained, including a series of knife-sharp ridges up to the summit, and it's not a great idea to be caught out by high winds on a ridge with a several thousand-metre drop on either side. Was Makalu about to evade me again?

Constantly watching the clouds rolling our way, we pressed on but just 50m below the summit I very nearly turned back. I was responsible for getting Dawa safely back down as well as myself, so I cleared my mind of summit fever and weighed up, in a completely logical way, the pros and cons of carrying on or going down. I decided that we could do it. We still had a chance. It was a calculated risk and I urged Dawa on to the summit.

The final ice rib was steep and I climbed up it carefully. One slip here and I would fall, pulling Dawa with me all the way to the glacier below. Dawa joined me on the ridge crest and, with drops of 3000m on my left and 1000m on my right, I led off along the final 60m knife-edged ridge.

Some summits, like Cho Oyu, are vast; others are the size of the average living room. Makalu's summit is about the size of a bar stool and Dawa and I had to take turns balancing on the top for the summit pictures. I could see the tiny dots of the Base Camp tents 3000m below.

Looking beyond Everest and Lhotse, through the storm cloud, I could see Menlungtse West, 7014m. In 1988 I had made the first ascent of that peak with Andy Fanshawe, on an expedition led by Chris Bonington. In the other direction, on the far eastern horizon and the border with India, I could make out Kangchenjunga, one of the three 8000ers that remained for me to climb. I anxiously watched the approaching storm but thankfully it never hit us and we were able to descend to the comparative safety of our bivouac without being hammered by hurricane-force winds.

It had been fantastic to be on top of Makalu with Dawa, his first 8000m peak. Sharing his jubilation on the summit made it all the more special. It was my 11th 8000er and my determination to climb the final three was now stronger than ever.

23 May 1999. The summit is about the size of a bar stool with dizzying drops of 3000m on all sides. I used my video camera to take a spectacular 360° point-of-view of my feet and the sheer drop as I shuffled round on the tiny, exposed summit.

DEALING WITH DEATH

Very few people have succeeded in climbing all 14 of the 8000m peaks. Most have either been killed or have retired after climbing just a few. Philosophically and psychologically I am coming to terms with the fact that I should also be dead by now, after taking part in 27 expeditions to climb 8000m peaks.

I have lost many friends and climbing acquaintances, not only on 8000ers but also in other climbing incidents on crags and mountains. Initially the frisson of death and danger must have attracted me. The adventure of climbing a huge, dangerous mountain was obviously much more serious than fell walking in England. However, I doubt that I initially realised I could be killed: 'It won't happen to me.'

It is possible that I over-estimated my skill level – most young people do especially if they also have a bit of good luck early on. Perhaps I did not even care, as I was hungry for the experience, thrill and excitement of climbing. Ernest Hemingway quipped that there are only three true sports: motor racing, bull fighting and mountain climbing. The rest are merely games.

Over the years I have had to come to terms with death and losing friends. Al Rouse's death on K2 in 1986 made me realise that even the best can perish. An 8000m peak is a very unforgiving environment. On my first climbing trip to the Polish Tatra mountains, in harsh winter weather, I remember the great mountaineer Voytek Kurtyka commenting that just to survive on an 8000er is a worthy challenge and should be success enough. Getting to the summit should never be the main objective. I developed my own philosophy: no mountain is worth a life, coming back is a success and the summit is only a bonus. I have a life wish, not a death wish. I climb to live life to the full, not to die.

Over the years, as I lost more and more friends, I could no longer push the risk to the back of my mind. I somehow had to accept that I might be killed. In 1995 I lost several friends – Alison Hargreaves, Paul Nunn, Paul Williams, Benoit Chamoux and Pierre Royer – yet carried on climbing. I became more aware of the risks, espccially on the giant 8000m peaks, but I accepted them. The dangers became more starkly obvious to me but I was still prepared to climb and enjoyed it. Psychologists might call it cognitive dissonance. I call it resilience: true Yorkshire grit.

The North Face. This was the first 8000er to be climbed (by the French in 1950 by a route up the crevassed slope on the right below the summit). It is a dangerous route exposed to serac collapse and avalanches. I climbed a new route up a slightly safer line further left.

12 ANNAPURNA

8091M, 2002

The weather in Kathmandu was worrying. Some of the most impressive thunderstorms I had ever witnessed had brought torrential downpours, deafening thunder and blinding lightning. There could be deep fresh snow on the mountain and an early monsoon. It was April 2002 and I was hanging out in Kathmandu arranging my permit to climb Annapurna. I have never enjoyed dealing with the bureaucracy of visiting tourism ministries or sorting out paperwork, usually delegating such tasks to an agent in Kathmandu, leaving myself free to organise logistics such as food and equipment, and planning the climb.

Eventually, most of the admin was complete and I intended to leave in the morning. It was my last night in Kathmandu before heading up to Base Camp. As I walked back to my hotel through the dark and rain-soaked streets, deep in thought, I tripped and fell heavily, cutting my arm badly. There were piles of rubbish and debris in the poorly lit streets and, stone-cold sober as I was, I had not been paying enough attention. The streets of Kathmandu are filthy and the risk of infection was high so my departure was delayed while I got my wounds cleaned and dressed.

Annapurna has a reputation as an avalanche-prone mountain. I did not want to research the fatalities on the mountain in detail but I knew that there had been about sixty deaths for a hundred ascents. Psychologically it seemed to me that I had a 60 per cent chance of getting killed once I left Base Camp. Truly a death zone. But I had no intention of letting that chilling statistic put me off. If the mountain seemed too dangerous I intended to use the expedition as an exploratory recce, to get a feel for it and then perhaps retreat and come back another season. Gung-ho is never a good attitude on an 8000m peak.

Funurbu, the expedition sirdar, helps porters across a dangerous part of the trekking path at 3700m. The trek to Base Camp on the north side of Annapurna is always arduous, with many steep, exposed sections. Sometimes ropes need to be fixed to safeguard icy snow slopes. The Kali Gandaki, the deepest gorge in the world, is far below the path in the clouds. This gorge separates Annapurna from Dhaulagiri and is older than the Himalayan peaks, pre-dating the tectonic uplifts that formed the great mountain chain.

In 1950, Annapurna had been the very first 8000m peak to be climbed, by a French expedition with no preliminary reconnaissance. Two climbers, Maurice Herzog and Louis Lachenal, reached the top in a gallant, brave push – but they suffered dearly for it. They used very light boots, Herzog's gloves were lost and they bivouacked high with only one sleeping bag. Their summit came at a terrible price – severe frostbite and gangrenous toes amputated by the expedition doctor on the return train journey through India. In his classic book *Annapurna*, Herzog recounts how all the pain, frostbite and amputations were worth it for the glory of France. Herzog talks about 'conquering' Annapurna and ends the book with the now-infamous and, to some, stirring words: 'There are other Annapurnas in the lives of men.' It's a great book but I will never understand how he can justify having fingers and toes amputated for the glory of France. All mine are important to me and I had no intention of donating any of my body parts just for glory!

Usually I set off on the trek from Kathmandu in late March to arrive in Base Camp in April, in good time for about 21 days' acclimatisation, before a summit bid in May. It was now well into April and I was still in Kathmandu with a trek to Base Camp of 10 to 12 days before I could even start acclimatising, never mind make a summit bid. The city was still being pummelled by heavy rain and I wondered how much fresh snow might be dumping on Annapurna, making my ascent even more avalanche-prone and dangerous. Heavy rain in Kathmandu does not always imply that the high peaks are plastered in snow – they lie far above the lowland pre-monsoon storms – so once my arm had healed enough, I set off hoping the rain would ease before I started the trek in.

I flew to Pokhara, a short drive from the road head where the trek starts. The first few days pass through villages in the Kali Gandaki valley, which narrows to a gorge further upstream. The rain fell unabated and I got a soaking every afternoon. Mornings would start crisp and clear. By 1pm the weather would begin to change and by 4pm every day it was pouring down. I made sure I started very early every morning and had my tent up by about 3pm. After leaving the last village in the main Kali Gandaki gorge, heading towards the north side of Annapurna, it was a five-day trek through the wilderness to Base Camp. High on the north-facing slopes, old hard winter snow covered much of the path. Some sections were exposed, and dangerously slippery, so hundreds of metres of rope had to be fixed to assist and safeguard the porters. We were climbing high above the Kali Gandaki gorge, the deepest valley in the world. Looking back I got my first good view of Dhaulagiri, one of my last remaining 8000ers. It reared up, a great white steep-sided fortress-like mass, a really impressive peak.

I enjoyed the views when it was not too cloudy or raining but still felt weak from the cut on my arm. It had turned a swollen, infected red-green and throbbed as I walked. I was on antibiotics and hoped that they, along with the fresh clean air, good food and exercise, would heal the infection before I needed to tackle the climb.

I arrived at Base Camp in a snowstorm on 26 April, my birthday. It felt like a good omen. An Indian Army expedition was already ensconced and welcomed me warmly. Their milky ginger and cardamom tea was a wonderful pick-me-up. Base Camp was in an airy, dramatic situation, perched on the edge of a hanging moraine with steep, soil-like cliffs falling 100m to the glacier. I knew Annapurna was not going to be easy and, that first night, it seemed to warn me as avalanches roared down all night long, like extra loud storm waves crashing on a beach. A particularly powerful one dusted the camp with powdery clouds of spindrift, like ash from an erupting volcano.

When the snow stopped, the wind increased. The following night the whole camp was nearly destroyed by hurricane-force winds blasting down from Annapurna. I had experienced such nocturnal katabatic winds before on Everest and K2. You hear them approach, sounding like an express train for several nerve-wracking minutes, then they hit the tents with a roar like a tornado ripping through

anything in its path. One of my Base Camp tents was destroyed but I managed to save all my climbing equipment.

After two nights' rest, my arm was healing well, the katabatic winds had stopped and I decided to push on up to Annapurna's treacherous North Face. Funurbu, a Nepalese climbing friend from a few years ago, had joined me to try to make a lightweight, fast Alpine-style first ascent of a new line on the left hand side of the vast North Face. The original French route of 1950 took a meandering line up the middle of the face and I felt my variation, up ribs and buttresses, would be less prone to avalanches and therefore safer.

After arriving at Base Camp, it is usual to spend up to three weeks acclimatising, going higher up the mountain in stages with rests in between to get used to the altitude before making a committing summit push. Such a strategy reduces the chance of contracting serious Acute Mountain Sickness (AMS), especially High Altitude Pulmonary or Cerebral Oedema (HAPE or HACE). Every acclimatisation trip on Annapurna, however, increased the chance that I might be avalanched on the fickle peak. My daughter, Fiona, was taking her final International Baccalaureate exams and I felt that worrying about her Dad being on Annapurna might affect her results. So I opted for a high-risk strategy of climbing Annapurna in one push, without any preliminary sorties. If I got stuck in a storm high up, I would be completely unacclimatised and probably die quickly. On the other hand, I would be spending less time on that dangerous mountain. It was a big risk but a calculated one.

The decision meant setting out from Base Camp with huge rucksacks weighing more than 30kg, as getting to the top and back might take as many as five nights. Monitoring Funurbu and myself for symptoms of AMS like a hypochondriac, I climbed higher up the face. I felt that I knew my body and how extreme altitude affected it, but I also knew that I was pushing my physical and mental boundaries with very little margin for safety.

On 5 May Funurbu and I moved to the final bivouac at 7000m. We would have to leave there at midnight to make a summit bid, so to save weight decided not to take a sleeping bag. I knew I could not spend two nights at that altitude.

No place to linger. Taking a break before climbing over the bergschrund and up a vertical ice pitch on to the ice face. Threatened by seracs teetering overhead which could collapse at any moment, this is a dangerous place to stop. Noticing the avalanche debris littering the snow here, I tried not to think about the consequences of any seracs breaking off and crashing down.

With or without a sleeping bag I would probably die, as I was not sufficiently acclimatised. I had a bitterly cold fitful rest, melting snow for drinking water and rubbing my toes to keep the circulation going and help prevent frostbite. Just after midnight, we set off on the final 1000m ascent. The route was mainly on snow and ice with some steep sections through ice cliffs and a 50m rock band just below the top. I reached the band as the weather started to break. Clouds rolled in and light snow started to fall. Undaunted, I assumed it was the usual pre-monsoon weather pattern of afternoon precipitation and climbed on, reaching the summit at about 11.30am on 6 May. I was on the summit of Annapurna, the tenth highest mountain and the first 8000m peak to have been climbed. It was the first British ascent of this mountain for 32 years. No Brit had stood on the summit since two of my early climbing heroes, Don Whillans and Dougal Haston, in 1970.

Funurbu came up to join me. I leant over and hugged him briefly before flopping down in the snow on the edge of a cornice overhanging the 2500m South Face. It had been an anxious, tense Alpine-style ascent in deteriorating weather and I had tested my limits of acclimatisation and endurance. I felt humbled that I had made it to the top of the notoriously dangerous mountain so quickly.

6 May 2002: On the summit after climbing a new line on the North Face, the first British ascent in 32 years. Holding a picture of Fiona and wearing a Royal Marines commando cap but no gloves!

Descending Annapurna into a cloud inversion

Fingers of fear tried to infiltrate my brain as the light snow turned to a steady fall. Visibility had disappeared and the 1000m slope back to the bivouac at 7000m was becoming loaded with fresh snow, making it more avalanche prone. After 15 minutes on the summit, taking the usual photo with my picture of Fiona, it was time to descend. The worsening weather made it increasingly difficult to find the descent route and, by early afternoon, we were in a full whiteout, fresh snow covering our ascent tracks. It was seriously bad weather and Funurbu was becoming agitated. He was not used to such conditions, whereas I am often out in grim, near-whiteout snowstorms on Scottish hills. Nevertheless, I knew that our predicament was dire and it was imperative that we pushed on down. Stopping at that altitude was not an option. Our chances of survival looked slim.

I tried not to show my concern as I broke trail in what I felt was the general direction of the bivouac, expecting to be engulfed by an avalanche at any moment. It took around five hours to fight our way back to the shelter of the tiny bivouac tent. We had left it at midnight and it was now 4.30pm. We both collapsed and huddled into the tent – dehydrated and exhausted but also relieved, happy and satisfied, especially once a couple of pans of snow had been melted for water, tea and juice.

The weather cleared for the night, the temperature dropped to -30°C and I desperately tried to prevent my fingers and toes freezing as I shivered away the bitterly icy darkness hours without a sleeping bag. It was self-inflicted torture. Although coughs are common at altitude I tend to look after myself and I do not usually get them. Now I had contracted a severe hacking and persistent high-altitude cough, probably from pushing hard in the dry thin air. It might not sound like much but at altitude a cough can be exhausting and climbers have been known to cough so hard that they break a rib or cough up the lining of their larynx. There was no chance of sleep. It was purely a matter of surviving a very cold, uncomfortable night, squashed together in the tiny, dark tent.

Thankfully the next day dawned fine. We packed all our equipment and headed down. It was slow going in the deep fresh snow and several steep sections had to be abseiled.

A group of Indian climbers at 6800m, waiting to abseil down the North Face.

Abseil descent on the North Face. Funurbu slides down the rope. Dhaulagiri 8167m can be seen across the Kali Gandaki.

Further down we had to dodge a fusillade of rocks melted out of the ice by the strong sun. On the way up that same dangerous section I'd narrowly missed being smashed by two rocks the size of cannonballs.

I had hoped to reach Base Camp that evening but we were slowed down by waiting for lulls in the rock fall and by the dangerous, unstable state of the sun-softened snow. Benighted, we arranged a hasty improvised bivouac on a rocky ledge. We were only a couple of hours from Base Camp and could see the tent lights winking at us. I was happy and could now relax, as I knew we were safe, out of

reach of rock falls and avalanches. I savoured the delights of an open bivouac, enjoying the expansive Himalayan night sky, the Milky Way and seeing several shooting stars.

It was still early May and I had climbed Annapurna in a very fast, record time. Normally an 8000m peak takes more than 30 days to climb from Kathmandu. It had taken me only 19 days from Kathmandu to the summit and I had made the first British ascent for 32 years via a new route, lightweight and Alpine-style. Annapurna had proved benign and I was content. Now only two 8000m peaks remained for me to climb.

Wearing my one-piece red 'Hinkes Suit', a loose windproof overall made out of Gore-Tex, at 7000m on Nanga Parbat. Diamir valley and Base Camp 3000m below.

DRESSED TO SURVIVE

Cold is an obvious danger on an 8000m peak. Extreme temperatures of 40 below can be encountered and -25°C is common. On rare windless days, the sun can burn exposed skin and heat up the thin air but protecting yourself from the cold is the greater challenge.

Layering is the best way to stay warm as still air, trapped between layers of clothing, provides insulation. It's also versatile. As it becomes colder you add more layers, removing them as you warm up. The objective is to stay relatively cool and comfortable. Too many layers will make you overheat and sweat. I usually wear a next-to-skin layer, a middle layer of fleece and, on an 8000m peak summit push, a down suit covered with what has been dubbed a Hinkes Suit.

A down suit is essentially a sleeping bag made into an insulated boiler suit with a hood. The Hinkes Suit worn over the top is a wind- and waterproof, breathable, light and loose-fitting overall which I designed as an extra layer of outer protection. It has copious large pockets in which to stash minimal equipment for a summit push, such as bottles of water, snacks, cameras and spare gloves. Both suits have full-length zips to allow ventilation, toilet functions and ease of getting on and off.

Gloves and mitts help prevent frostbitten fingers. Usually, I also wear thin gloves as basic insulation and to protect my hands from burning sunlight. Toes are easily forgotten and many climbers suffer frostbite and have to have their toes amputated. I wear clean, loop stitch, high wool content socks inside plastic boots. Clean socks and clothes are warmer and I often keep back a fairly new pair of socks for maximum insulation and warmth on a final summit push.

Years ago, heavy leather boots with sheepskin inners were the norm. Now plastic outer boots with modern closed-cell foam insulating inners are warmer and lighter. I usually wear one size bigger on an 8000er, to allow for any swelling of the feet, and thicker socks. The extra room enables me to wriggle my toes to keep the circulation going and prevent frostbite.

High-altitude boots look very similar to one another, especially when you are exhausted and suffering the effects of altitude. I mark a large 'L' and 'R' on mine, to make it simpler to identify and pull them on without wasting brainpower. Some have poked fun at the idea but have been converted once they've tried it, appreciating the simplicity and effectiveness when you are tired. My French friends were convinced and marked theirs 'G' et 'D'.

The human body acts like a chimney, with heat rising and escaping through the head, so headwear is very important. I wear a thin balaclava with a thicker one over the top when it is colder, as well as the down-filled hood on the one-piece suit. As we say in Yorkshire: 'Don't go without your bl***y hat'.

13 DHAULAGIRI

8167M, 2004

Crampons scratched and skittered on the wind-blasted, grey-brown rock slabs as I scrambled to the bare, exposed summit of Dhaulagiri. It crossed my weary mind that this was my 13th 8000er, leaving only one more to climb if I got back down in one piece; but perilously steep, dangerous slopes had to be descended before I could regain the safety of Base Camp. It felt like I was in one of the most inhospitable, barren, bitterly cold places on Earth. I could not face filming, photographing or even savouring the moment. I just wanted to leave the hostile, windswept, rocky summit. I noticed that a piton had been hammered into a crack on the summit. Somehow I pulled myself together to take a few photos and film a couple of short pieces on the highest point.

Pasang Gelu, my climbing partner, took out two Buddhist prayer scarves and unfurled them into a strengthening wind that almost tore them from his grip. I forced myself to get out the summit photo of my daughter Fiona, with my new grandson, Jay, and snapped a couple of photos across the Kali Gandaki to Annapurna and beyond to Manaslu. I tried to take more pictures for one of my sponsors but the wind whipped their logo away. I took the hint that it was time to descend and set off down, crampons scraping the rock like fingernails on a blackboard.

Just below the summit ridge, a gully leads down to an avalanche-prone snowfield that we now had to traverse. Pasang and I had left a rope in the gully to help us abseil down. Facing in and climbing down would have been possible but not as fast or as safe. At the very top of the gully, the body of a climber was laying face up on the rock. He had been there for ten years. I looked at the well-preserved corpse, still clothed and with crampons attached to his boots. He lay on his back, as if sunbathing or resting,

The view of Dhaulagiri from Base Camp. The route goes between the ice fall and the 750m rock face plastered with snow on the true left bank of the glacier. It goes under this dangerously loose wall to the col on the left and continues up the skyline ridge left to right. It's a lot steeper than this photo suggests and this glacier approach is exposed to massive avalanche and rock fall risk. Many climbers have been engulfed and killed here and most are never found. Tragically my friend Pasang Gelu was buried in an avalanche here, while helping a Japanese expedition.

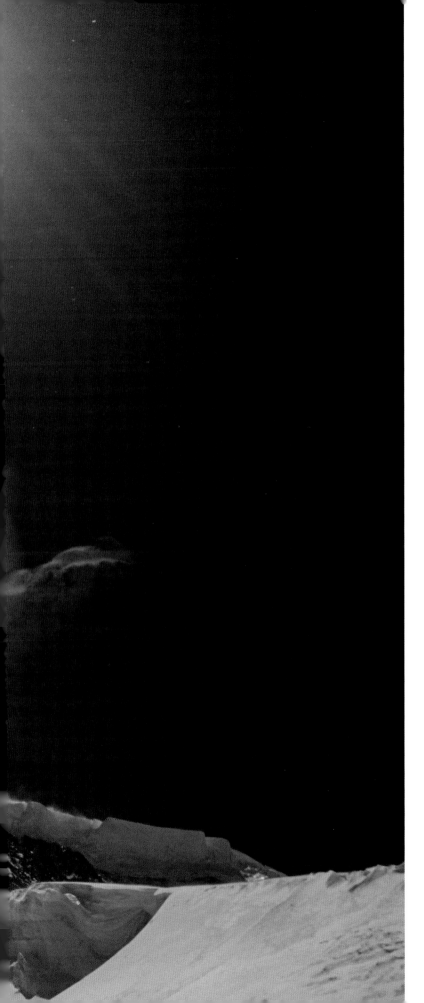

about to get up and climb on. Seeing a body like that is always a grim shock and reminder of our mortality.

Pasang and I had left Base Camp three days earlier, on 14 May 2004, without any great expectations of reaching the summit. Fresh heavy snow covered hard, steep ice slopes, making conditions dangerous and difficult.

We had been acclimatising in Base Camp for more than three weeks but I judged that the poor snow conditions on the mountain and prevailing bad weather meant that we only had a five per cent chance of success.

About 40 minutes from Base Camp, the route traverses beneath an unstable 750m cliff face packed with loose cannonball-sized rock artillery that regularly strafes the route. A helmet is really only a token gesture of defence against rock fall like that and you do not want to commute such a route more than is absolutely necessary. Further on, the way continues up a glacier in a deep valley formed by Tukuche Peak on one side and Dhaulagiri on the other. Many climbers have been killed on those lower sections of Dhaulagiri. Massive seracs larger than the white chalk cliffs of Dover tower above. If an avalanche breaks off the

Left

Digging a ledge for a tent at the
foot of the North East Ridge 6400m.

upper slope there is little chance of escaping it. You are in a trap. Avalanche debris is spread liberally across the glacier, huge mounds of snow and ice blocks the size of cars. It is a sinister, unnerving place, through which it is best to keep moving to reach a safer zone.

It took seven hours to climb from Base Camp to a flat bivouac spot at 5900m. The afternoon glare from the sun, concentrated in the crucible-like glacier bowl, seemed to drain all my power and energy. The lack of oxygen and the heat and glare reflected off the snow were enervating. When afternoon cloud built up bringing shade and snowfall, it was a welcome relief. Pasang and I relaxed in our tiny tent diligently melting snow on the gas stove and drinking tea, coffee and powdered orange and nibbling at our food rations.

All too soon it was morning. We took nearly five hours to push up to 6400m, and there we dug a ledge into the 45° icy snow slope to pitch our tent and again spend the afternoon and evening horizontal, resting, trying to conserve energy for the summit push and descent.

On 16 May we left for our final bivouac at 7400m. This 1000m climb took nearly ten hours. To speed progress and make our rucksack loads lighter, I decided not to take the sleeping bags. The strategy had worked for me on Annapurna and, anyway, we would be leaving well before dawn the following day and not really sleeping at that altitude. On the steep, bare ice en route to the bivouac I noticed a couple of bodies on small ledges to one side of the route. One was half-wrapped in ripped tent fabric. Pieces of discoloured and ragged equipment, including rucksacks,

Opposite

Campsite at 6900m. In the
foreground are Nilgiri (7061m)
and Tilicho (7134m), with
Annapurna (8091m) behind.

jackets, sleeping bags and ropes, lay around. I climbed on, focusing on the task in hand, and eventually reached a spot on which we could just about pitch our small tent.

Up at 7400m, it took a lot of Herculean digging to scrape out a ledge, which even then was only big enough for three quarters of the tent. Squeezing inside and snuggling up together, we did not have much time to miss our sleeping bags as we kept ourselves busy constantly melting ice and snow in a tiny pan over a mini gas burner. The air temperature was well below freezing but the sun's rays hitting the tent warmed the inside slightly. As the sun set the temperature dropped like a stone. It became dramatically cold, probably -30°C. Now I definitely missed my sleeping bag. I lay in the dark and thought about how good the weather had been for the past three days and how serious it would be for us if it deteriorated now, trapping us here at 7400m in sub-zero temperatures without sleeping bags.

By 9pm, I was really struggling to keep warm. In the cramped confines of the tent I wriggled and massaged my toes all night long to prevent frostbite. Pasang was just as busy with his own feet. Sleep was out of the question. Across the Kali Gandaki I could see that Annapurna was engulfed in a massive thunderstorm. Bright flashes of lightning were lightening up the sky but there was no sound – it was too far away. It was like watching a silent film. Seeing the primeval power of the storm was fascinating, half of me was enjoying the show, but my interest in it was tempered by the knowledge that we would undoubtedly perish if the storm moved over and engulfed Dhaulagiri. In the confined space of the precariously perched tiny bivvy tent, at -30°C, it was just a matter of suffering and surviving until setting off at 2.30am.

My new LED head torch cast a soft white glow around me, hollowing out the gloom as I climbed the firm snow and rock slope in darkness. It was comforting, in a sort of 'head under the blankets, let's not think what's out there' sort of way. I emptied my mind of fear as I climbed on, preparing myself for the 800m, ten-hour slog to the top. I knew that by the time we returned it would be late in the afternoon.

The climb was going to be a committing Alpine-style summit push, just the two of us, alone on Dhaulagiri.

After less than an hour of climbing my toes were cold. They were beginning to freeze and felt solid. I contemplated returning to the tent to warm them up but instead I stopped on some rocks on the snow slope and took my boots off to massage my feet. As the blood began to flow again and circulation returned to my toes the pain of the hot aches became excruciating but at least it indicated that my toes were still alive. Masochistically, I enjoyed the pain of knowing my toes were okay. I am prepared to suffer some pain, just not amputation.

Pushing on, we reached the upper snowfield hanging above a mind-boggling 3000m-drop to the glacier. The slope was hard packed wind slab with some patches of soft snow and I was not happy about the avalanche threat. My senses were urging me to retreat. I felt there was a 50 per cent chance it would slide. I became anxious. We were so near the top, and going down would mean the end of any chance of reaching the summit. I would have to return another season. I was scared but, overriding my rational survival urge to go down, I dug an avalanche pit, a little trench in the snow deep enough to allow an examination of the various layers. There was definitely some instability in the snow pack but I revised my estimate of the likelihood of avalanche, convincing myself now that it stood at only ten per cent.

Somehow, at the time, that level of risk seemed acceptable and I decided to carry on. I explained my thinking to Pasang and gave him the option to go down. He decided to carry on with me. It took nearly three hours to cross the snow slope. I was breaking trail and on the edge of fear for all that time, expecting to hear the distinctive boom as the slope broke away, sweeping us down 3000m to the glacier.

By 9.30am it was warm enough in the sun to strip off the top half of my down suit, even though the air temperature was still well below freezing. With no wind and the strong sun it could have almost passed for a pleasant Alpine day, if we hadn't been gasping for breath in the thin air and expecting to be avalanched. By 11am my subconscious mind flickered slightly and warned me that the weather conditions were on the turn. The rising wind signalled change and I put my down suit back on. I felt sure now that we would make the top but was less confident about how far back down we might manage to get in the deteriorating weather.

Around midday we emerged from the final gully on to the bare, rocky summit ridge. As if to quash any rising sense of triumph, I caught sight of the corpse that marked the top of the gully. The summit was only 10 or 15 minutes away, a scramble over wind-scoured slabs to a bleak and unwelcoming final lump of rock. As soon as I reached it I was anxious to get down. It was no place to linger. After a few quick photos I was back at the top of the descent gully and quickly abseiled down to the snowfield. Traversing back across it, Pasang and I were so tired that we took rests clipped to our ice axes which were rammed into the snow as anchors. I noticed that the summit above had disappeared in thick cloud. 'We're in for it,' I thought, as the inclement weather quickly set in.

The wind had strengthened and scudding cloud had enveloped us by the time we got back to our bivouac at 7400m. We dived inside and spent another night without sleeping bags, clinging to the inside to stop the tent being ripped from the ledge by the buffeting wind. By daylight we were worn out but so happy to have survived. We summoned reserves of stamina and energy, and by nightfall had made it slowly and carefully down to 5900m. We had our sleeping bags now but were still another day away from Base Camp.

The summit, 17 May 2004, holding a photo of Fiona and Jay. Across the Kali Gandaki, Annapurna is hidden behind my body. Dhaulagiri is the rockiest 8000m summit I have stood on, the summit seems to be swept bare of snow. I found a piton in the summit rocks and wondered who had hammered it in.

Some of the most dangerous ground still had to be crossed, including the traverse beneath the 750m unstable cliff only 40 minutes from Base Camp. After reaching the top and risking all those avalanche-prone slopes we might still be killed so close to safety. Thick mist shrouded the lower route as we descended. Any avalanche or rock fall would come unseen out of the thick murky cloud. All we could do was climb on down in the eerie twilight and hope fate would be kind to us.

Once on the flat glacier I knew, even in the misty gloom, that we were safe. I shared a happy, exhausted sigh of relief with Pasang and set off in the direction of the milk tea, egg, chips and chapattis I knew would be waiting in the haven of Base Camp. Dhaulagiri was done.

THE INCIDENT PIT

There is danger in mountaineering. Any complacency can lead to a serious accident, even close to home. When I started hill walking in Britain there were no mobile phones. Were you to trip and break a leg, you might have a long wait before a mountain rescue team arrived. Should the weather be poor, exhaustion and exposure could lead to hypothermia, even death.

Any rock climbing has the risk of falling off but for winter and Alpine climbing the risks, which include avalanche and frostbite, are greater. In the Himalaya, especially above 8000m, the dangers are magnified again; simply surviving becomes a challenge in itself.

As a mountaineer you are always skirting around and trying not to slip into the 'incident pit'. Small, seemingly unimportant incidents or minor nuisances can accumulate and become a major problem. For example, when setting out on a winter climb you might forget your spare gloves. That is not a problem if you do not drop your main pair. If you do you will not be able to climb as efficiently and might suffer frostbite. Similarly, a punctured water bottle could result in dehydration and further impairment of performance and decision making.

An accumulation of such small errors or accidents can lead to near misses or even a serious incident. The 'incident pit' is an imaginary hole into which you slide deeper with every setback, until it is difficult to escape.

Ultimately you are in so deep that extricating yourself becomes impossible and you die.

Constant evaluation of your situation, controlling or modifying the effects of any minor incidents, is vitally important. On any 8000m peak you are already on the edge of the pit, probably with at least one foot dangling over. The safety margin is already compromised and it is easy to slip deeper as you continue towards the summit. Exhaustion, dehydration, changing weather and avalanche conditions are all factors that must be constantly checked to ensure that, once on the summit, you have sufficient energy for the descent and remain in control of the situation.

Attention to detail can mean the difference between life and death. If you feel you are sliding further into the pit you must take measures to scramble back up, metaphorically speaking. And you must always be prepared to accept turning back from a summit if necessary.

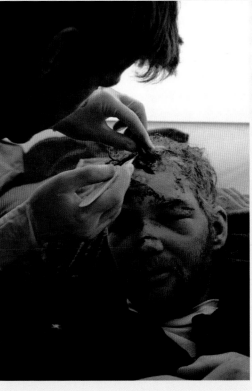

Top right

Rick Allen after being avalanched high on Makalu.
He was swept 400m from the top of the slope,
over the rock slabs. When I reached him he was
semi-conscious and covered in blood. Somehow I
improvised a rescue and struggled down with him.

Right

He's alive. Back in Base Camp on Makalu at
5700m – Doc cleans his head wounds.

14 KANGCHENJUNGA

8586M, 2005

All my senses tore at my oxygen-starved brain, screaming 'full-on red alert'. I was at my limits, alone, hypoxic and fatigued at 8000m, striving to get to the summit of Kangchenjunga. Spindrift was streaming down the steep snow slope. My feet were cold, my toes nearly numb, frostbite inexorably creeping into them after many hours immersed in the deep freezing snow, plugging steps. Sometimes I sank thigh-deep in the fresh snow as I pushed on up higher into the death zone.

It was dangerous – perhaps hopeless. A sea of boiling white cloud swirled upwards, encasing me in tendrils of mist. The summit, glistening in the clear blue sky above seemed to entice me on. I was in a quandary. Should I climb on? With luck I might stay above the bad weather ceiling and the weather might clear. Yet the churning cloud kept pace as I climbed higher, engulfing me. My senses had been on overload for so long I was beginning to think irrationally. I forced myself to override the desire to push on. It would have been suicidal. Retreat was the only option.

Descending into the thick cloud I managed to find my tiny bivouac tent at 7600m. Exhausted and almost spent, I knew that I must not stop there. If the storm worsened I could be trapped and would perish from having been too high, too long. However much I needed a rest, I had to continue to a lower altitude, out of the death zone.

As it happened there was no choice. As the snowstorm strengthened, spindrift avalanches cascading down the face were burying the tent. The situation was getting ever more serious. About a metre of fresh snow had already fallen, conditions were near whiteout and only three hours remained before darkness would overtake me. I contemplated holing up in the tent but that could have meant being entombed by

The massive 3000m South Face, from the moraine-covered Yalung Glacier near Oktang. The route starts at the bottom of the face and traverses up right to the Great Shelf. From there it goes diagonally left up the ramp above the sickle-shaped cliff to the col and back right below the ridge to the summit. The top is set back so it does not look like the highest point.

spindrift; logically I knew that it was imperative to get to a lower altitude to survive.

It took me nearly four hours to descend 500m, something that would usually have taken less than an hour. I found a flattish spot and set up my tiny bivouac tent at 6900m in darkness. All night the scouring wind ripped and battered the fabric, spindrift noisily scratching the nylon like particles from an industrial sandblasting machine.

Next morning I took stock of my situation. There were still 900m of perilous, insecure snow to descend to reach the relative safety of a ridge spur at 6000m known as the Hump. After that came 700m of steep and hazardous slopes to Base Camp. As I set off the wind picked up and spindrift lashed my face, ice particles stinging my eyeballs, making it difficult to see. To protect my eyes, I put on goggles but could still see little more than 20m ahead.

The descent was becoming an epic and I sensed that I was slipping into what I term the 'incident pit', a dangerous crater that leads to the point of no return – death. Once you dip your toe into the 'pit' you can get swiftly sucked in before you realise, many separate little problems combine and escalate until you are out of control. I was dehydrated, weary and beyond hunger and my body was consuming its reserves. As I slowly and painstakingly descended, I was wading waist-deep in snow, sometimes crawling through drifts and over flimsy snow bridges that were spanning deep icy chasms. Twice, snow bridges over crevasses collapsed and I sank in up to my chest. My heart seemed to pop out through the top of my head.

As I tentatively stepped on to another crevasse bridge across a yawning void, some 2m wide but 50m deep, instinct tipped me off that it was about to collapse and I threw myself at the opposite side. There was a loud, sharp, brittle crack, like metal breaking. I thought my ice axe or crampons had snapped as they bit into the steel hard ice of the crevasse wall, then realised it had been my left arm that had made the snapping sound and was no longer working properly.

I struggled, kicked and flailed my way out of the crevasse, narrowly avoiding the fall into its icy depths. For a while I just lay on the lip thinking that I was now well into the incident

pit. Pain stabbed at the crippled arm but I was thankful that I had escaped falling into the crevasse. In a Monty Python way I thought, 'Well, I've still got one working arm and two good legs, and I haven't broken my expensive new ice axe!' I felt lucky that it was not my leg or knee that had been damaged and at least I could still walk.

It took several more painful hours to struggle down to Base Camp in the dark using my head torch. I arrived at about midnight and was soon drinking restorative milk tea as well as choking back a strange mix of emotions. I had escaped from the incident pit by a close shave. I was incredibly fortunate to be alive and thoughts crammed my brain like a rock concert crowd behind a locked turnstile. Tomorrow I would admit them entry, one by one; but for now I rested and savoured a single sensation – damn, this tea tastes good.

It was five years before I was high on Kangch again. It was 2005 and my very last 8000m peak, 50 years on from the first ascent by Joe Brown, George Band, Tony Streather and Norman Hardie. Its summit is only a few metres lower than K2's and, after my previous experience, I knew that Kangchenjunga would be a serious and dangerous final test, a

Above

The top camp at 7600m, in 2000, with Jannu 7710m, Makalu and Everest in the far distance. The tent is dug into a ledge hacked out of the snow slope. Later in the season I made a solo push for the summit from here.

Opposite

Porters at 4900m on the Yalung Glacier near Oktang, heading towards the 3000m South West Face. This was an arduous two-day trek. We had to break trail through deep fresh snow, after a big snowstorm that had held us up for three days in Ramze and Oktang.

fitting finale. It felt like a gnarly old friend waiting for me. My plan was for a lightweight two-man ascent, just my old mate Pasang and me, as on Dhaulagiri; a tried and tested friendship and team. However, Kangch turned out to be a near-death experience yet again, perhaps a too-grand finale. By chance I had left possibly the hardest mountain until last. Although K2 is always considered first prize, Kangchenjunga is only 14m lower. It is a much vaster peak with wide, exposed avalanche-prone slopes and difficult rock climbing above 8000m. The trek to Base Camp takes 12 days including a two-day section ferrying loads across the glacier to a high Base Camp. Leaving the UK in late March, trekking in during April, I planned on making a first summit bid between 5 and 10 May but that season's weather was particularly grim. Some acclimatisation sorties were made up the mountain but I had to hang on in camp until the end of May before I could make a summit bid.

By 29 May, Pasang and I were bivouacked at 7400m, planning for the summit on 30 May. It had taken three days to reach that point, climbing a new variation line Alpine-style with heavy rucksacks in difficult, varied and steep terrain. I had hoped to reach 7600m but deep snow had thwarted us, so now we faced a 1200m climb to the summit. That is a big push; by comparison, on Everest there is only 500m on the north side or 900m on the south side from the South Col. On K2 the shoulder is at nearly 8000m, leaving only 600m to climb to the top. I knew we would be in for a hard time and that it would be touch and go.

On 30 May we set out at 1.30am, hoping to summit by midday, giving plenty of daylight time in which to descend. It turned out to be a 26-hour climb during which Pasang would retreat, leaving me to a solo summit push and a desperate, almost terminal descent alone in the dark.

It was extremely hard going all day but the weather was reasonable, some wind, some cloud and temperatures of about -20°C – not too bad for extreme altitude and the best we could hope for with current weather patterns. I could see the summit ridge most of the time, taunting me, enticing me towards it. By then I had made my mind up that I was going to keep on going until dark, although I knew midday was a more sensible turnaround time on any 8000m peak.

Pasang and I climbed together up the Sickle, a steep ice and snow ramp leading to the col left of the summit ridge. Just below that the route cut diagonally right across more difficult mixed rock, ice and snow. Some of the holds were loose. This was real climbing at over 8000m and so, so dangerous.

Afternoon clouds were building. Pasang decided to go back. Nothing much was said. He just accepted that I wanted to carry on and he set off down. There was no way I could follow him. I had to push on. I could feel myself taking more risks than usual, perhaps because this was my last mountain and without doubt one of the hardest. It was not a snow plod; there were vertical rock steps to climb. Fortuitously I had found pieces of 6mm cord left behind the previous year by an Indian Army expedition, which I cut up and attached to the rock face to help on the descent. Finding this old, thin rope slowed me down, but I knew that it could mean the difference between life and death on my descent. At over 8500m this was the highest rock climbing that I had ever done, and I tried to appreciate it as I scrambled tentatively over the light coloured rock. The geologist in me even wondered what sort of rock it was.

By 6pm the clouds that had gathered to the south west were already engulfing the summit. I knew I was in for worse but still pushed on into the swirling clag and wind. In the hill fog visibility dropped below 30m. I grew more determined and kept going. In the back of my mind I knew that I could die and yet I was not prepared to do so. I concentrated on the task in hand and suppressed the overwhelming anxiety in my hypoxic brain. Continuing on over the bare rock and pulling up on holds carefully, as some were loose, I tried to

recognise the crack that Joe Brown had climbed in 1955. I am sure I noticed it and traversed below it to pull up onto a rocky platform close to the top.

Night was encroaching fast. It was about 7.15pm and it would be dark within 20 minutes. I stopped about three metres short of the summit, out of respect to the local Sikkim people who regard Kangchenjunga as a sacred mountain. I took the usual photo of myself with a picture of Fiona and Jay, my daughter and grandson, holding the digital camera at arm's length.

That was it. I had done it. Before moving on I recorded a short piece to camera allowing myself a choking, gasping,

Opposite

Traversing and trying to avoid huge crevasses on the Great Shelf at 7000m. Jannu 7710m lies behind.

Left

Looking up from the Great Shelf at 7000m to the ramp and the summit. Nasty clouds are lurking behind the summit ridge.

Summit of Kangchenjunga, 30 May 2005, holding a photo of Fiona and Jay. The coating of rime ice on my face shows the extreme weather conditions. It was getting dark and my new digital camera proved its worth, capturing this image at arm's length with fill-in flash. Even as I took this, I was thinking that it might be the last ever photo of me and that, being digital rather than film, it would be recoverable. This was on the 50th anniversary of the first ascent in 1955 by Joe Brown and George Band.

croaky cheer into the video camera, wondering whether those would be my last ever spoken words.

As a grand gesture, in worsening weather and encroaching darkness I climbed the final few metres to the very top of Kangchenjunga and straddled the Nepal–India border. Retaining my respect for the people of Sikkim, I trod lightly.

To stand any chance of survival I then had to descend at least 1200m. With snowfall and wind intensifying I set off down in the dark, trying to convince myself that it was only like a winter night exercise in the Cairngorms. It wasn't. I suddenly lost the ability to block out my fear and the brutal reality of my situation hit me. I was alone in the dark at 8500m, in a blizzard on Kangchenjunga, third highest mountain in the world. Suddenly I was scared. I was acutely aware of the enormity of my predicament; I started gasping, hyperventilating and shaking like a leaf. It was a panic attack, brought on by the stark realisation that I was quite likely to perish and had only myself to thank.

'Shit, this is serious,' I remember mumbling to myself. 'I've had it. I'm not going to get away with it this time.' No rescue team would be able to help; no helicopter was going to pluck me off. I was in the death zone and if I let my guard down I was a goner. I was well and truly slipping into an enormous 'incident pit'.

I had to pull myself together, convince myself I could descend to the relative safety of the bivouac below. I have plenty of experience of climbing in the dark but here the fresh snowfall was building up a massive avalanche potential. I pushed this fear and anxiety to the back of my mind – if it had overwhelmed me I would have been out of control – and I focused on the task of surviving and not falling off as I down climbed the steep face. I had no option but to press on. I had to find the best route down and concentrate on climbing technique. I thought of Benoit Chamoux and Pierre Royer, my French friends who had disappeared here, and Wanda Rutkiewicz who also perished here. Would I be next, swallowed up by the storm-bound mountain?

With a grim relish I attacked the situation. This was now an epic and nothing else mattered but getting myself out of my self-made predicament. I felt confident that I was capable, I was determined to survive and knew I had 30 years of stamina and skill to draw on. I had the will to live.

Climbing down the rocky steps and walls, facing in much of the time, I was vividly reminded of the seriousness when I pulled a loose hold off. It clattered away into the abyss of the southwest face. Concentrating only on the climbing, my mind began to relax. Abject fear dissipated, like shrugged-off flakes of snow. I was no longer scared. It was uncanny. I was experiencing a heightened sense of pleasure and enjoyment, as if I had left my physical body and mentally and spiritually, in a very intense way, was actually enjoying the near-death experience.

Panic attacks do not get you down a mountain. I had taken control of the situation and pulled myself together. And now life was simple. Get down to safety, or die.

Often my crampons would throw up tiny showers of sparks in the darkness as the metal scraped the bare rock.

It was difficult to see in the persistent snowfall, as my head torch beam reflected back off the snowflakes.

Sometime in the night I caught up with Pasang. Relief and joy flooded through me knowing he was still alive. Digging deep into our last reserves of stamina, we struggled on down together, reaching the bivouac at 3am on 31 May. It had been a 26-hour epic. We were almost spent and very dehydrated.

After slowly melting snow for water and taking a fitful rest, we continued down for another day and a half towards the welcome haven of Base Camp and tea, egg, chips, chapattis, *dal bhat* and a satellite phone call to assure Fiona that I was safe.

Drinking and savouring the simple pleasure of milk tea in Base Camp, it began to sink in that I had climbed all the 8000m mountains. I was free. I was finished with 8000m near-death experiences. Free simply to enjoy the hills.

Above
The last couple of metres to the summit.

Left
Looking down from the summit of Kangchenjunga, almost in the dark, on 30 May 2005.

There have been joys too great to be described in words,

and there have been griefs upon which I have not dared to dwell;

and with these in mind I say: Climb if you will, but remember

that courage and strength are naught without prudence, and that

a momentary negligence may destroy the happiness of a lifetime.

Do nothing in haste; look well to each step; and from

the beginning think what may be the end.

Edward Whymper, *Scrambles in the Alps*

Roseberry Topping in the North York Moors: where it all began

ROSEBERRY TOPPING

Known locally as the North Yorkshire Matterhorn, Roseberry Topping is one of the most distinctive and iconic hills in Britain. It is only 320m high but what it lacks in height it makes up for in charm and profile, with a superlative 360° panorama from the summit.

This conical hill with a steep rock face is a Jurassic sandstone outlier of the North York Moors. As a young boy, the sight of the mini-mountain would thrill me as we drove past, usually on the way to the seaside. I remember noticing the tiny white spot – the painted Ordnance Survey trig pillar – on the top, and the Lilliputian clusters of people crawling over the summit. It influenced me in those childhood days. It seemed like a giant, almost perfectly formed mountain to my young mind and I wanted to climb it. I did not get the chance until I was in my teens but now I go up it several times a year.

It can easily be tackled in less than an hour, longer if you choose to meander around its slopes. From the top the view is a contrasting mix of wild moorland and industry. The heather, a resplendent purple in August, stretches east towards Whitby; south, the Cleveland Hills escarpment snakes into the distance; west, the Pennine fells and the distinctive squat outline of Penhill and the Yorkshire Dales can be seen; to the north lies the River Tees estuary with huge bulk carrier cargo ships lurking in the North Sea; and below stretches the industrial might of the steel works and chemical plants of Middlesbrough and Teesside.

The great Yorkshire explorer James Cook went to school in nearby Great Ayton between 1736 and 1740 and climbed Roseberry Topping many times. I am sure that it must have helped fuel his passion for exploration and adventure. He went on to sail around the world, exploring and mapping. He was the first European to land in Australia and made extensive explorations of the Pacific but was killed in 1779 on Hawaii, in a dispute with natives.

In spring and early summer Roseberry Topping has some beautiful expanses of bluebells on its lower slopes but a bimble to the top of the mini-Matterhorn is a pleasure any time of the year, one that I appreciate all the more after surviving the 8000m peaks.

AFTERMATH

He is lucky who, in the full tide of life, has experienced a measure of the active environment that he most desires. In these days of upheaval and violent change, when the basic values of today are the vain and shattered dreams of tomorrow, there is much to be said for a philosophy which aims at living a full life while the opportunity offers. There are few treasures of more lasting worth than the experiences of a way of life that is in itself wholly satisfying. Such, after all, are the only possessions of which no fate, no cosmic catastrophe can deprive us; nothing can alter the fact if for one moment in eternity we have really lived.

Eric Shipton, *Upon That Mountain*

Main photo

The Mi-17 Russian-built helicopter in Ramze 4500m. It embodied the sight, sound and smell of freedom. Mi-17s are not the safest means of transport, but it meant a one-hour flight instead of a five-day yomp out and I felt I deserved a lift home after Kangch, my final 8000m peak.

Inset photo

With Pasang and Base Camp kitchen staff at Kathmandu airport after the helicopter lift back to civilisation.

The distinctive throb of a Russian-built Mi-17 helicopter heralded freedom.

I was at Oktang, little more than a flat area at 4800m in the ablation valley above the Yalung Glacier, with impressive views back to the south west face of Kangchenjunga. On the trek-in, more than a month earlier, I had been holed up here in a snowstorm for several days and had wondered whether I could reach Base Camp. Crevasses on the glacier had been covered by deep, fresh snow. Route finding had become difficult and it was very dangerous for porters to continue. I had had to sit out the snowstorm and wait for the snow to settle before laboriously breaking trail and finding a safe route up the glacier to Base Camp.

All that seemed like something from another life as we bundled our equipment into the helicopter and scrambled

Above

Stupa on top of the Boudhanath Temple, Kathmandu.

Above right

Signing the Everest summiteers' board of fame in the Rum Doodle restaurant/bar Kathmandu. Climbers who reach the top of Everest are eligible for free meals in this restaurant.

on board. I was looking forward to a warm shower, a good meal, a clean bed and a cold beer in Kathmandu.

After climbing Kangchenjunga and surviving its avalanche-prone descent, I had rested and recovered in Base Camp for a couple of days. My time was spent eating, drinking and making satellite telephone calls to family, sponsors, friends and the media. Eventually I made the trek of several hours down to Oktang, low enough for an Mi-17 helicopter to land, pick up Pasang and myself with our kit and fly us back to Kathmandu. We waited two days for the weather to allow the lumbering but very welcome Mi-17 to fly in.

The interior is basic, with none of the padding you find in western helicopters and simple bench seats around the sides, leaving plenty of space for cargo to be piled in the middle. Crews usually comprise two or three Russians with a Nepalese co-pilot. The Russian pilots are very experienced, some having survived combat and mountain flying in Afghanistan. Mi-17s are not, however, the safest mode of transport and crashes do happen. Even in the most modern helicopters, flying in mountain areas is dangerous, especially

if the weather socks in and it becomes cloudy. As one veteran Russian pilot dryly told me: 'We have to be very careful flying in the clouds. Around here, they are full of rocks.' I pushed any thoughts of rock-filled clouds to the back of my mind and enjoyed the scenic flight to Kathmandu, which took about 90 minutes. It was a lot quicker than a five-day trek out.

It felt wonderful to be back in Kathmandu after climbing Kangchenjunga, my final 8000er. I felt a sense of freedom – to get on with enjoying my life and my climbing – and contentment but not really relief. Climbing all the 8000ers had not been a chore. If anything, I was somewhat sad that it was over. I had enjoyed pushing myself close to destruction and testing my resilience on the highest and most dangerous mountains.

I had no desire to rush back to the UK. I wanted to enjoy myself and chill out in Nepal. I was keen to see my daughter, Fiona, with grandson Jay, and they flew out for a holiday with me in Kathmandu. The British Ambassador held a celebratory reception in the British Embassy – a nice surprise – and some friends from Britain even flew out to join us. A large Himalaya-shaped cake had been prepared and, as well as the ex-pats, many of my Nepalese friends were invited to the British Embassy reception.

It felt good to be alive and relish the Nepalese way of life for a few days with Fiona, Jay and my climbing friend

Pasang. I even visited a few of the tourist attractions such as the famous temples, and took a sightseeing flight to Everest. Two-year-old Jay had a great time, as there are plenty of colourful sights, noises and smells in Kathmandu, and the Nepalese love children.

Returning to Britain, I was proud to be made an Honorary Citizen of my hometown, Northallerton, with a reception at the Town Hall in the High Street. Many friends and old schoolmates turned up. I was flattered when my old grammar school, now Northallerton College, instigated an annual award: the Alan Hinkes Award for Endeavour which is now presented annually to a deserving young person.

It was a refreshing change not to have to think about organising another expedition for a while and I was looking forward to enjoying a spring season in Britain. I had been away on climbing expeditions between March and June for much of the previous 18 years. Now, I looked forward to appreciating bluebell woods in springtime, rock climbing, hill walking in the UK as well as just having fun with Jay and Mia, my grandchildren, instead of a two or three-month expedition.

Some people have suggested that the hills of home must have paled into insignificance after all the expeditions and Himalayan climbs I have been on but, after more than 50 expeditions, I can honestly say that I still get great pleasure and enjoyment from a day out in the British hills.

I have climbed all over the world, mostly lightweight, Alpine-style, including a lot of first ascents, and filmed many documentaries. My expeditions include North and South America; the Andes; Africa; the Greater Ranges of the Himalaya and Karakoram, including India, Pakistan, Nepal, Tibet; Tien Shan; the Middle East and the Arctic, as well as 27 trips to the 8000m peaks. I have climbed the highest, whether it is Everest, Chimborazo or Mauna Loa, and also been to the lowest point on the planet, the Dead Sea. After all that 'expeditioning', I still have an adventurous streak and will continue to travel abroad.

There are also many nooks and crannies, hills and dales in Yorkshire and the north of England waiting for me to explore and enjoy. There are the Wainwrights to climb – fells named after the famous and dedicated Lakeland mountain author in the sublimely beautiful landscape of the English Lake District. I might even 'compleat' the Munros, the 282 Scottish mountains over 3000ft. There is a lifetime of mountain enjoyment to be had in Britain.

In 2006 I was awarded the OBE by Her Majesty the Queen at Buckingham Palace. When I stepped forward I think I was possibly as nervous as I have ever been on an 8000m peak.

Left

Winter in the Scottish
Highlands – the Aonach
Eagach ridge, Glen Coe.
(© *Trail Magazine*)

The fact that I am still alive, when so many friends and others climbing the 8000ers have died is humbling. In some sense I am coming to terms with the idea that I should be dead by now. It might sound dramatic but the 8000ers could just as easily have exterminated me as they have many other mountaineers. It is only death that has stopped many mountaineers from achieving the full tally of 14.

I can never give up climbing. I still enjoy being out on the lower hills, mountains and rock and ice climbs in Britain as much as ever. Ironically I have had a few near misses in the British hills and try to avoid complacency on any climb. One such incident occurred on a Lake District winter climb when I escaped a lethal wind slab avalanche. After solo climbing a steep ice pillar, I exited onto an easy-angled snow slope. As I continued up it released, sweeping me back towards the edge of a 200m-drop. My mountaineering survival instinct immediately clicked in and I knew that I only had a second or two to react. I somehow rolled out of the avalanche a split second before plummeting over the edge. It was a salutary reminder not to underestimate any climb, or let complacency creep in, no matter how much fun you are having.

Abroad, many challenges remain on the bigger mountains. Thankfully there are thousands of unclimbed mountains in the world, mostly between 5000m and 6000m in height. Many are not difficult and many are unnamed. I made the first ascent of a 5300m mountain in central Asia and was pleased to be able to name it Peak Fiona, after my daughter.

Other challenges that interest me include the Seven Summits. As a geographer I would find it interesting to visit the seven continents to climb the seven highest mountains in

Opposite

Nanga Parbat: a climber works his
way up the Kinshofer Couloir at
4800m. Later in the day as the sun
melts the ice, rocks are released
and the ensuing stone fall and
avalanches can turn this couloir
into a death trap. A Japanese
climber was killed by rock fall here
in 1998. Base Camp can just be
seen on a patch of grass at the side
of the Diamir glacier 600m below.

Pasang Gelu prepares to descend from the sloping bivouac platform at 7400m on Dhaulagiri. We had spent two nights here without sleeping bags, spending the second night, after descending from the summit, holding on to the tent to prevent it and us from blowing away. If we had been bivouacking in the open as I did on Shisha Pangma, I doubt that we would have survived. Without the protection of a small bivouac tent the wind chill would have killed us. Base Camp is in the cloud inversion over 2000m below.

the world. I have already climbed most of them and I am looking forward to a couple of mini-expeditions to climb the remaining few.

I have been back to Everest since climbing the 14 and might return there again. Nothing, however, could persuade me to climb the 8000m peaks again. They are all too dangerous. Even if I were offered an enormous fee to guide K2, Kangchenjunga or some other 8000er, I would not accept it. I climbed those mountains for myself, not for money so why would I risk my life now for money? The only two 8000m peaks I would consider climbing again are Cho Oyu and Everest but there are many other mountains I want to climb, as well as treks in the foothills I'd like to enjoy.

I do have a tentative plan to enjoy some exciting but less dangerous challenges. One such, already completed, was reaching all the highest points of the 39 traditional English counties in one week. It was interesting and fun, if a little tiring. I used the event to raise funds and awareness for Mountain Rescue England & Wales. It was fascinating to travel to parts of England I would not normally visit, such as East Anglia, where there are very few hills.

My adventurous activities do not just revolve around climbing. As well as cycling, canoeing and kayaking, I have

With Mountain Rescue.

enjoyed plenty of testing underground excursions exploring the caves and pothole systems beneath the Yorkshire Dales.

In 2012 I was picked as an Olympic torchbearer, both an honour and an interesting – if brief – experience. I might even take my Olympic torch up Scafell Pike, the highest mountain in England.

I now have two grandchildren, Jay and Mia, and a future challenge could be to take them up a few British hills. I would never encourage them to climb an 8000m peak, but just to enjoy an English hill or a Yorkshire fell walk.

Essentially I have done what I wanted to do. Anything else will be a bonus.

Left

The Great North Run for charity.

Centre

Training on a bike in the Margalla Hills above Islamabad. It was very hot and humid and it made sense to cycle up the steep hairpin bends in the relative cool of early morning. I was probably cycle fit enough for a Tour de France stage by the end.

Right

With Jay and Mia.

Shooting the summits

In landscape photography, mountains represent the pinnacle of the art. From across the vast range of features on the Earth's surface, mountains stand as symbols of power, of human aspiration, of permanence and of danger, the realm of the gods. For photographers it's a theme that can last a lifetime, as I know from experience.

A good mountain photograph can be obtained without climbing a mountain but as soon as a photographer becomes a little more ambitious, trekking distances into the mountain landscape, the challenge rises exponentially. Ambling a few flat miles with a camera may be no problem but add in the gear required for an overnight or two and a few thousand metres of ascent and descent and suddenly photographing mountains becomes a serious and athletically challenging experience.

But this is nothing compared with high-altitude mountaineering. The logistical challenge alone is utterly daunting, and the priority of survival in some of the earth's most hostile conditions to life is absolutely paramount. It is really quite astonishing that photography is even considered by mountaineers, especially in the brutally thin air of the high Himalaya and Karakoram. It is a tribute to Alan's artistic instinct that he remained committed to his photography when he really should have been concentrating 100 per cent on staying alive.

Knowing how difficult it is to use a camera in winter conditions, even at modest altitudes in Scotland, I cannot begin to imagine how hard it is to do so at over 8000 metres. Here every breath is a gasp, the wind roars remorselessly, the air temperature is way below freezing, the light is intense and extreme, and the photographer-mountaineer must struggle with gloves, goggles and risk frostbite while operating an instrument designed to work at room temperature and at sea level. Taking a picture of any kind is an achievement.

Alan Hinkes is not only one of a tiny band of elite mountaineers to have climbed all the world's highest mountains, he can also make genuinely artistic judgements and tell proper stories with his photography. His mountaineering skill has enabled him to ascend and descend safely while still taking great photographs, and his devotion to photographic duty is clear, never more so than in his iconic image from the summit of K2.

It is just before sunset and the shadow of the mountain seems to reach to infinity. This crystallised moment is an image sublime in its scale and terrifying in its significance. Having endured the ordeal of struggling to this apex of the world, Alan must now descend from the summit of the world's second highest mountain (and one of the most deadly), in rapidly gathering darkness.

And he did descend safely, from every single one of these epic adventures, so that we can now share at least some of the visual wonders he encountered. His photographs are both a moving documentary record, and artistic expression, of what it means to encounter the highest places in the world.

JOE CORNISH

At sunset K2 casts a gigantic shadow across the Karakoram, into China and India. The shadow is poking above the horizon, possibly because of atmospheric haze, and I am on the apex of that shadow taking the photo. Other summits are, left to right, Gasherbrums I, II, III, IV and Broad Peak, Pakistan.

The 8000m Peaks and their First Ascents

Peak	Height in metres and feet	Country	First ascent	Date of first ascent
Everest	8848m/29,028ft	Nepal/China	Edmund Hillary, Tenzing Norgay	29 May 1953
K2	8611m/28,250ft	Pakistan/China	Achille Compagnoni, Lino Lacedelli	31 July 1954
Kangchenjunga	8586m/28,169ft	Nepal/India	Joe Brown, George Band (Tony Streather, Norman Hardie)	25 May 1955
Lhotse	8516m/27,940ft	Nepal/China	Fritz Luchsinger, Ernst Reiss	18 May 1956
Makalu	8463m/27,766ft	Nepal/China	Jean Couzy, Lionel Terray	15 May 1955
Cho Oyu	8201m/26,906ft	Nepal/China	Joseph Joechler, Pasang Dawa Lama, Herbert Tichy	19 October 1954
Dhaulagiri	8167m/26,795ft	Nepal	Kurt Diemberger, Peter Diener, Nawang Dorje, Ernst Forrer, Albin Schelbert	13 May 1960
Manaslu	8163m/26,781ft	Nepal	Toshio Imanishi, Gyalzen Norbu Sherpa	9 May 1956
Nanga Parbat	8125m/26,660ft	Pakistan	Hermann Buhl	3 July 1953
Annapurna I	8091m/26,545ft	Nepal	Maurice Herzog, Louis Lachenal	3 June 1950
Gasherbrum I (Hidden Peak)	8068m/26,470ft	Pakistan/China	Andrew Kauffman, Pete Schoening	5 July 1958
Broad Peak	8047m/26,400ft	Pakistan/China	Fritz Wintersteller, Marcus Schmuck, Kurt Diemberger, Hermann Buhl	9 July 1957
Shisha Pangma	8046m/26,397ft	China	Hsu Ching with nine climbers	2 May 1964
Gasherbrum II	8035m/26,360ft	Pakistan/China	Fritz Moravec, Joseph Larch, Hans Willenpart	7 July 1956

APPENDIX 2
ALAN HINKES EXPEDITIONS

Date	Mountain	Expedition
1982	Mount Kenya, Kenya, East Africa	Diamond Couloir ice climb and Hell's Gate rock climbs
1982	Mount Meru, Tanzania, East Africa	Solo trek and rocky scramble to summit
1983	Kilimanjaro, Tanzania, East Africa	Heim Glacier solo snow and ice climb
1984	Everest, Himalaya, Tibet	Reached 7100m+ on Tibet side, Rongbuk North Face
1984	Kulu, Himalaya, India	Dharmsura (White Sail) (6000m peak), new route, Alpine-style
1985	Cordillera Blanca, Andes, Peru	New routes (5000m and 6000m peaks), Alpine-style
1985	Kulu, Himalaya, India	New route, Dharmsura West Face (6000m peak), Alpine-style
1986	Kishtwar Himalaya, India	Alpine-style expedition
1987	Tatra mountains, Poland	Difficult winter ascents
1987	Denali (Mount McKinley), Alaska, USA	West Buttress climb to summit and Cassin Ridge attempt
1987	Shisha Pangma, Himalaya, Tibet	New route/first ascent of central couloir line up North Face, Alpine-style. First 8000er
1987	Lhotse South Face, Himalaya, Nepal	Big Wall Climb to 7900m+, with Polish team
1988	Tatra mountains, Poland	Winter ascents. Big mountain routes in very cold conditions
1988	Menlungtse, Himalaya, Tibet	West Face to West Peak (7000m peak). New route/first ascent, Alpine-style
1988	Makalu, Himalaya, Nepal	Reached 8200m+ Alpine-style, before avalanche and rescue of injured climber
1989	Manaslu, Himalaya, Nepal	First British ascent South Face/Pillar, Big Wall climb. Second 8000er
1990	Cho Oyo, Himalaya, Tibet	Expedition ascent, solo to summit. Third 8000er
1990	Shisha Pangma, Himalaya, Tibet	New route/first ascent, North Face couloir line, Alpine-style to Central Summit
1991	Everest, Himalaya, Tibet	Reached 7000m+ on north side, Tibet
1991	Broad Peak, Karakoram, Pakistan	Expedition, guiding client to top. Fourth 8000er
1992	Nanga Parbat, Himalaya, Pakistan	Mazeno Ridge attempt and Schell Route. Reached 7200m+ before rock fall injured climber and retreat
1993	K2, Karakoram, Pakistan	Reached 7800m before rescuing injured climber on South East Ridge
1994	K2, Karakoram, China	North Face/Ridge. Reached 8200m+, retreat due to high avalanche risk
1995	Makalu, Himalaya, Nepal	Injured leg on approach, hospitalised
1995	K2, Karakoram, Pakistan	Summit, solo from 6500m, Alpine-style. South East Ridge. Fifth 8000er
1996	Everest, Himalaya, Tibet	Summit via North Ridge. Cameraman. Sixth 8000er
1996	Gasherbrum I, Karakoram, Pakistan	Solo ascent. Seventh 8000er
1996	Gasherbrum II, Karakoram, Pakistan	Solo ascent via South Face. Eighth 8000er

Date	Mountain	Expedition

At this point I realised that I had climbed eight 8000ers – just over half – and just six remained. Only a handful of mountaineers had climbed them all. I decided to go for all 14.

Date	Mountain	Expedition
1996–1997	Ecuador	Climbing volcanoes, including Cotopaxi (5000m peak) and Chimborazo (6000m peak), highest mountain in world measured from centre of Earth to summit
1997	Lhotse, Himalaya, Nepal	Solo West Face Couloir via Khumbu Icefall. Ninth 8000er
1997	Makalu, Himalaya, Nepal	Retreat from 7800m due to avalanche risk and approaching monsoon
1997	Nanga Parbat, Himalaya, Pakistan	Retreat, back injury. Slipped disc
1998	Nanga Parbat, Himalaya, Pakistan	Kinshofer route, Diamir Face. Tenth 8000er
1999	Makalu, Himalaya, Nepal	Lightweight two-man ascent. Eleventh 8000er
1999–2000	Israel	Rock climbing, and visiting the lowest point on the planet
2000	Kangchenjunga, Himalaya, Nepal	Retreat from 8000m due to avalanche risk. Fell in crevasse, broke arm
2001	Kilimanjaro, Tanzania, East Africa	Trek, Mount Meru and Kilimanjaro
2001	Mauna Kea and Mauna Loa, Hawaii, USA	Highest mountain in the world measured from its seabed base
2001–2002	Aconcagua, Argentina	Highest mountain in Latin America
2002	Annapurna, Himalaya, Nepal	Fast lightweight two-man ascent. New route on North Face. First British ascent for 32 years. Twelfth 8000er
2002	Tien Shan, Central Asia	First ascents of previously unclimbed 5000m+ peaks. Named one Peak Fiona, after my daughter
2003	Oman, south west Asia	New rock routes
2003	Kangchenjunga, Himalaya, Nepal	Retreat: poor weather and infection
2004	Morocco, North Africa	New routes, rock climbs
2004	Dhaulagiri, Himalaya, Nepal	Lightweight two-man ascent. Thirteenth 8000er
2004	Atlas Mountains, Morocco, North Africa	Mount Toubkal, highest peak in Atlas range
2005	Kangchenjunga, Himalaya, Nepal	Lightweight two-man ascent. New variation line on South West Face. British ascent on 50th anniversary of first ascent. Fourteenth and final 8000er

The list continues after 2005. I will never stop climbing.

Follow me on Twitter: @alanhinkes.

Alan Hinkes

I have climbed the three contenders for the title of the highest mountain on Earth. Everest is the highest above sea level, Chimborazo has the greatest distance from the centre of the Earth to its summit, and Mauna Kea has the greatest height from its base to the summit. I have also been to the lowest point on the planet, the Dead Sea. Perhaps this combination is a 'first', just for fun.

APPENDIX 3
GLOSSARY

Abseil (rappel) Controlled descent using a rope.

Alpine Mountainous region, originally the European Alps.

Alpine start Early morning, pre-dawn start.

Alpine-style Lightweight, self-supporting mountain climbing.

AMS (acute mountain sickness) Illness that affects people at altitudes above 2500m, caused by lack of oxygen and low air pressure.

Arête Sharp rugged mountain ridge produced by glaciation.

Ascender Mechanical clamping device used to ascend an anchored rope.

Bergschrund Large crevasse, very deep and wide, formed at the top of a glacier where it is separating from a snow slope. Often used by climbers to describe a randkluft, which is the gap between the ice of a glacier and rock face.

Bivouac (bivvy, bivi) Lightweight camp using minimal shelter out in the open, or a small tent.

Cairn Man-made pile of rock, sometimes marking a summit or path junction.

Carabiner (karabiner) Metal, usually alloy, loop or clip with a spring-loaded gate through which a climbing rope can be threaded.

Col The lowest point between two peaks.

Cornice Wind-sculpted snow or ice overhanging a ridge or mountain face.

Couloir Gully.

Crampons Steel spikes that attach to climbing boots providing reliable traction on ice.

Crevasse Slot in a glacier surface. Crevasses vary in width and depth and can be hidden by surface snow.

Fixed rope Rope anchored to a route by the lead climber and left in place for others who follow.

Glacier Mass of permanent ice, flowing like an extremely slow river.

Glissade Sliding down a snow slope under control.

HACE (high altitude cerebral oedema) Swelling of the brain due to fluid increase, a serious form of altitude sickness.

HAPE (high altitude pulmonary oedema) Fluid build-up in the lungs, serious altitude sickness.

Headwall Steep section of a mountain face.

Hypothermia Condition when your body core temperature drops below normal.

Steep rock and mixed climbing at over 7700m on the north side of K2. Very taxing at this altitude.

Hypoxia Deprivation of oxygen to the human body.

Ice axe Mountaineering tool, used to assist a climber on snow and ice. With a spike at the base of the shaft and a metal head consisting of a pick and an adze.

Icefall Broken, generally unstable and dangerous area of a glacier, usually with huge ice towers, often larger than a house.

After the storm. Looking down the Yalung Glacier, Kangchenjunga.

Karabiner See Carabiner.

Lead To be the first climber on a pitch or section of a climb.

Mixed climbing Combination of snow, ice and rock terrain.

Moraine Accumulation of boulders, rocks and soil deposited by a glacier. A *lateral* moraine forms along a glacier; a *medial* moraine forms in the middle; and a *terminal* moraine at its snout.

Névé Hard, icy snow.

Nut Metal wedge jammed into cracks for protection.

Penitentes Pinnacles of snow and ice on a glacier. They can be a few centimetres to several metres high.

Pitch Section of climbing on a route.

Piton Metal spike or peg that can be hammered into rock cracks.

Rappel (abseil) Controlled descent using a rope.

Rime Layer of ice coating rock and objects.

Runnel Groove in rock, snow or ice.

Saddle Mountain pass or col.

Scramble Easy climbing.

Scree Broken rock, boulders and stones at the base of a cliff. Sometimes called talus.

Self-arrest Ice axe braking; using your ice axe to stop a fall.

Serac Huge block of ice, often larger than a house.

Sirdar Expedition foreman.

Snow stake Length of angled alloy hammered into the snow as an anchor.

Spindrift Fine wind-blown snow and ice crystals.

Spur Ridge protruding from a mountain.

Traverse Moving laterally across terrain rather than ascending or descending.

Verglas Thin coating of ice on rock.

Whiteout Weather condition, where white cloud merges with white snow causing the horizon to be eliminated. It can cause disorientation.

INDEX